THE COMPOSITION OF CONSUMER SAVINGS PORTFOLIOS

Studies in Consumer Savings

Studies in Consumer Savings, No. 3

CONSUMER SAVINGS PROJECT
INTER-UNIVERSITY COMMITTEE FOR
RESEARCH ON CONSUMER BEHAVIOR

THE COMPOSITION OF CONSUMER SAVINGS PORTFOLIOS

Henry J. Claycamp

PUBLISHED BY THE BUREAU OF ECONOMIC
AND BUSINESS RESEARCH · UNIVERSITY
OF ILLINOIS · URBANA · MAY 1963

PREFACE

This monograph is the third in a series of technical reports presenting findings of the Consumer Savings Project of the Inter-University Committee for Research on Consumer Behavior. The previous publications in this series have presented methodological results of the project. This is the first monograph to present results relating to consumer savings behavior.

The focus of this study is on the composition of consumer portfolios. Its objectives are to throw light on the frequency of ownership of different types of portfolios, to attempt to explain different patterns of ownership, and to explore the interaction among the ownership of different assets. In the course of doing so, Dr. Claycamp presents a thought-provoking hypothesis on the composition of consumer portfolios which could have far-reaching effects on the analysis of consumer finances.

Future monographs in this series will present further results relating both to consumer savings behavior and to the methodology of consumer financial surveys. A summary volume on the methodological aspects of the project is currently in process.

This project has been financed by a grant from the Ford Foundation, with supplemental assistance from the United States Department of Agriculture. Financial support for additional work currently under way has been provided by the National Science Foundation and by the United States Department of Labor. Robert Ferber, Research Professor of Economics at the University of Illinois, is director of the project.

The members of the Inter-University Committee for Research on Consumer Behavior are:

Lincoln Clark, New York University, Secretary-Treasurer
Robert Ferber, University of Illinois
Raymond Goldsmith, Yale University
George Katona, University of Michigan

v

Theodore Newcomb, University of Michigan
James Tobin, Yale University
Guy Orcutt, University of Wisconsin, Chairman

The monographs in this series are research reports. The Inter-University Committee, as sponsor of this research, makes every effort to ensure both the quality of the reports and their orientation toward meeting a real need. Nevertheless, the findings reported in this way summarize conclusions arrived at by project staff and do not necessarily represent the individual or collective views of the members of the Inter-University Committee.

GUY ORCUTT, *Chairman*
Inter-University Committee
for Research on Consumer Behavior

ACKNOWLEDGMENTS

The author wishes to express his gratitude to Professors R. W. Mayer and T. A. Yancey of the University of Illinois who read early drafts of the monograph and made many helpful comments and suggestions. He also wishes to thank Professor Stanley Steinkamp of the Consumer Savings Project and the University of Illinois who, while acting as sounding board for ideas both good and bad, also had a beneficial influence on the final product. Above all, the author wishes to acknowledge the invaluable guidance and assistance of Professor Robert Ferber, Director of the Consumer Savings Project, which were instrumental in the development and completion of this study. The study was made under a fellowship granted by the Ford Foundation and the author also wishes to acknowledge this support. However, the conclusions, opinions, and other statements made here are those of the author and not necessarily those of the Ford Foundation or the individuals mentioned above.

HENRY J. CLAYCAMP

Champaign, Illinois
March 19, 1963

CONTENTS

LIST OF TABLES

LIST OF CHARTS

PART ONE

INTRODUCTION

I. THE NATURE AND SCOPE OF THE PROBLEM

The Problem

Although governmental agencies, business organizations, and independent academic researchers have been subjecting consumers to ever increasing scrutiny, comparatively little information is available about one important aspect of consumer behavior, i.e., consumer savings behavior. In particular, little reliable information is available about the present composition of consumer savings portfolios and the factors which determine how consumers hold their accumulated savings.[1]

Savings as an Economic Variable and the Need for Statistics

This lack of information about savings behavior is not attributable to a failure on the part of economists and others to recognize consumer savings as an instrumental economic variable. The importance of savings and the need for adequate statistics is widely discussed in economic and business literature. A particularly lucid explanation of the problem was given by Raymond Goldsmith in his statement to the Subcommittee on Economic Statistics of the Eighty-fourth Congress.

The importance of savings statistics for the analysis of short-term economic fluctuations or business cycles stems from the fact that saving needs to be offset smoothly and continuously by new investment if an interruption of the circuit flow of income is to be avoided, an interruption which would result in a decline in national income and the volume of production, and which might lead to a cumulative downward movement in the economy. We must therefore have up-to-date information on the volume of saving as well as the volume of investment, its forms and flows.

---

[1] It should be made clear at the outset that the terms "savings" and "portfolio" have a broader meaning in this study than they have in commonly accepted financial usage. In financial terminology, "savings" usually refers to the amount of funds held in highly liquid assets such as savings accounts or government savings bonds. Here, savings refers to the total value of the assets held in any form by the consumer unit. Similarly, in financial usage, the term "portfolio" designates the list of transferable financial assets held by an individual or by an institution. In this study, the term designates the complete list of assets (both financial and physical) and debt holdings of consumers. This use of the term is not unique to this study. For example, see Survey Research Center, *1960 Survey of Consumer Finances* (Ann Arbor: Braun-Brumfield, 1961), p. 117.

The main purpose of statistics of savings in long-term analysis is to help understand the process by which economic growth, and particularly the expansion of the country's stock of capital is financed. This requires estimates of saving separately for the main groups that habitually make funds available and those that absorb them, and in addition statistics in as much detail as possible of the flow of these funds from savers through financial intermediaries to investors.

The third of the main uses of statistics of saving is more technical, but by no means less important — the current analysis of the capital market. This use . . . is of interest primarily to institutions active in the capital market, such as investment bankers, insurance companies, and investment companies; and to the government agencies that are closely connected with developments in the capital market, such as the Treasury, the Federal Reserve Board, and the Securities and Exchange Commission and the Council of Economic Advisers.[2]

This statement explains clearly the importance of the need for accurate data on the form, flow, and the amount of saving, as well as on the form and amount of total savings in general.[3] Since consumers regularly hold a large proportion of total assets of the economy and provide a major proportion of gross national saving, the importance of the consumer sector can readily be seen.

Influences of Consumer Decisions About Portfolio Composition

At any given time, consumers who have accumulated funds are faced with many alternative ways of holding those funds. They may hold only currency, or they may invest the funds in different kinds of financial and/ or physical assets. The economic and financial impact of savings held in each of these forms is markedly different.

Moreover, shifts in the flows of funds within the financial and physical asset categories can exert important influences on financial institutions, economic and financial conditions in general, and on the consumers themselves. If the net result of many consumer decisions regarding the composition of their portfolios is a shift away from liquid, fixed-dollar assets such as government savings bonds and savings accounts to variable-dollar assets such as stocks, important forces are released.[4] The decrease in funds going to institutions providing fixed-dollar claims stimulates them to competitive activity in an attempt to spur consumer demand. In many

---

[2] U.S. Congress, Joint Economic Committee, Subcommittee on Economic Statistics, *Reports of Federal Reserve Consultant Committees on Economic Statistics*, 84th Cong., 1st Sess., 1955, pp. 228-29.

[3] The distinction between saving and savings is important. Saving is the flow concept and savings is the stock concept. Thus, saving is the amount added each period to the total stock of savings. This study is an investigation of savings rather than of saving.

[4] A fixed-dollar asset is one which is not subject to fluctuations in market value. Thus the owner of a fixed-dollar asset has claim to a specified number of dollars. A variable-dollar asset is one which is subject to fluctuations in price. Thus, the number of dollars represented by the claim may appreciate or depreciate.

cases, these institutions are subject to severe legal restrictions as to the type and extent of competitive activity they can employ. Hence, they may be faced with a decrease in their incoming flow of funds which they can do nothing about and as a result they may have to alter other policies such as those dealing with prospective borrowers of funds. At the same time the increase of funds going into equities tends to push up prices of securities, stimulate the growth of institutions providing this type of investment (e.g., mutual funds), and make this type of financing more desirable to corporations.

If, on the other hand, the net shift is away from liquid financial assets to physical assets such as real estate and consumer durable goods, the effect is to stimulate demand in different sectors of the economy. In both cases, however, the effect on the individual is to reduce his liquidity position and make him more vulnerable to fluctuations in income and downward movements in prices.

These examples show the need for information about the composition of consumer savings portfolios and the factors which influence consumers to hold a given portfolio.

Objectives

The objectives of this study are threefold:

(1) to present an exploratory investigation of the composition of consumer savings portfolios;

(2) to present an explanation, based on economic and psychological theory, of why the structure is as it is; and

(3) to present guidelines and hypotheses for future research in this area.

The first objective can be divided into two major parts — the investigation of the combinations of holdings in the portfolios and the investigation of the fixed- versus variable-dollar nature of portfolios.

The major purpose of Part Two, in which attention is focused on the asset composition of portfolios, is to explore the interaction of assets. That is, the analysis is directed at determining the effect of the ownership of one asset or combination of assets on the ownership or amounts held in another asset or combination of assets. This analysis should show which assets are substitutes and which assets are complements in the minds of consumers. Information of this type is crucial to studies of demand for a given asset or portfolio of assets. For if the ownership of a certain asset or combination of assets affects the likelihood of ownership of a second asset, this effect must be specified in the models used to explain the demand for the second asset if one is to get unbiased and consistent estimates of the parameters. In addition, the nature of the interaction between assets may provide otherwise unobtainable information about the way consumers select portfolios.

The purpose of Part Three is to provide information about the fixed-versus variable-dollar composition of consumer savings portfolios and the factors which are associated with differences in this composition. As was pointed out before, this aspect of portfolio composition has important influences on financial institutions, general financial and economic conditions, and on the ability of the individuals to withstand fluctuations in income and changes in the price level. Yet little information is presently available on the factors which account for this type of variation in portfolio composition. In Part Three the analysis is directed at determining the relationship of this aspect of portfolio composition to various socioeconomic and psychological characteristics of consumers.

It should be stressed at this point that it is not the purpose of the study to investigate what determines *how much* consumers save, or variations in the amount of savings of different groups, or to provide a comprehensive description of the structure of the savings of consumers in general. Nor is it the purpose of the study to make judgments as to the optimal nature of actual portfolios, or to derive a comprehensive theory of choice to explain the actual portfolio composition. Rather, the purpose is to investigate two aspects of consumer savings portfolios — the interaction between assets in the actual combinations owned and the factors associated with the differences in the fixed- versus variable-dollar composition of portfolios — given that the consumer has a stock of funds and has alternative ways of holding those funds.

Sources of Information and Related Studies

Consumers are the only source of information of the type just described. It is impossible to use aggregate statistics obtained from financial institutions to derive distributions of consumer savings portfolios for different socioeconomic groups. Thus, the nature of the data needed implies some form of reporting of savings information by consumers. And currently, the only feasible method is by direct survey of a sample of consumers drawn from the population at large. However, consumer surveys are high-cost sources of information and they present especially complex problems when dealing with a psychologically sensitive subject such as individuals' savings. Consequently, relatively little information of this type is currently available.

In the following section a brief review of the major sources of information about consumer saving and savings is presented. With the exception of the Surveys of Consumer Finances, the data presented by these sources are not amenable to studies of consumers' portfolios. However, they are included because they are the main sources of statistical information on saving and savings which are available on a continuing basis, and they provide a check for the validity of aggregate estimates made from survey data.

In addition, the second part of the review covers major analytical studies of consumer savings behavior and their relation to the problem of portfolio composition. The section covers examinations of consumer savings in general and studies of specific components of consumer savings. The relationship of each investigation to this study is explained.[5]

Major Sources of Information

Personal Saving

The National Income Division of the Department of Commerce has provided annual and quarterly estimates of aggregate personal saving since 1942. The series has also been extended on an annual basis back to 1929. These estimates are derived using the income-residual approach, i.e., the difference between personal income, and the sum of personal consumption expenditures and personal tax and nontax payments. In addition to the saving of households and individuals living alone and in institutions, that of unincorporated businesses, personal trust funds, private pension funds, nonprofit institutions, mutual life insurance companies, mutual savings banks, savings and loan associations, and credit unions is included in the estimate of aggregate personal saving. Expenditures on consumer durables are considered as current consumption expenditures but expenditures on housing are not. The estimates are published regularly in the *Survey of Current Business* in the February, May, August, and November issues.

Saving by Individuals

Since 1942 the Securities and Exchange Commission has presented a series of estimates of saving by individuals. The balance sheet approach is used in preparing these estimates rather than the income-residual approach. However, there are some differences in coverage in saving by individuals and in personal saving. To reconcile the two series the SEC publishes a second estimate, "aggregate personal saving." The estimates of individuals' saving include the saving of unincorporated businesses,

---

[5] It is clearly beyond the scope of this monograph to present a comprehensive review of all of the literature in each of these fields. Consequently, with the exception of the major statistical sources, only those analyses which have relevance to the methodology or the results of this study will be presented here. For an excellent review of sources of statistics on saving, see Subcommittee, *op. cit.*, pp. 94-158. For a comprehensive bibliography of analytical studies of saving and savings behavior, many of which are based on the Surveys of Consumer Finances, see Survey Research Center, *op. cit.*, pp. 297-310.

trust and pension funds, most nonprofit organizations, credit unions, and some agricultural credit organizations. The series includes net increases in the following categories: (1) currency and bank deposits; (2) savings and loan associations; (3) life insurance reserves; (4) securities — governmental, corporate, and other; (5) liquidation of mortgage debt; (6) liquidation of other debt; (7) nonfarm dwellings; and (8) other consumer durables.

Saving in items 1 through 6 is called liquid saving or financial saving. The total saving in items 1 through 8 is called gross saving. The estimates are published quarterly in the SEC's *Statistical Bulletin* and in press releases entitled "Volume and Composition of Individuals' Saving." The best guide to the methodology used in compiling the series and its use is *Individuals' Saving* by Irwin Friend and Vito Natrella.[6] As is the case with the personal saving statistics published by the Department of Commerce, the savings by individuals series includes more than the saving of consumer units. However, it probably comes as close as any series based on aggregative sources.

Flow of Funds, Saving, and Investment

The Board of Governors of the Federal Reserve System first published their statistics on the flow of funds in the United States in the October, 1955, issue of the *Federal Reserve Bulletin.*[7] Since that time revisions have been made to make the series more amenable to studies of saving and investment and to make it available on a current basis.[8] The series now presents the flow of funds, saving, and investment for the following 11 sectors: (1) consumers and nonprofit organizations; (2) farm business; (3) nonfarm corporate business; (4) corporate business; (5) federal government; (6) state and local government; (7) commercial banking and monetary authorities; (8) savings institutions (mutual savings banks, savings and loan associations, and credit unions); (9) insurance companies and private pension plans; (10) finance not elsewhere classified; and (11) foreign transactions.

The following categories are used to trace financial flows through each of the 11 sectors:

(1) Gold and treasury currency
(2) Demand deposits and currency
(3) Fixed-value redeemable claims
  (a) time deposits

---

[6] New York: Wiley, 1954.

[7] Federal Reserve Board, "Flow of Funds in the United States, 1939-1953," *Federal Reserve Bulletin,* Vol. 41, No. 10 (October, 1955), pp. 1085-1184.

[8] See Federal Reserve Board, "A Quarterly Presentation of Flow of Funds, Saving and Investment," *Federal Reserve Bulletin,* Vol. 45, No. 8 (August, 1959), pp. 828-59, for a detailed description of the new series.

      (b) savings shares
      (c) United States savings bonds
  (4) Saving through life insurance
  (5) Saving through pension funds
  (6) Credit and equity market instruments
      (a) federal obligations
      (b) state and local obligations
      (c) corporate and foreign bonds
      (d) corporate stock
      (e) mortgages on 1- to 4-family properties
      (f) other mortgages
      (g) consumer credit
      (h) security credit
      (i) bank loans not classified elsewhere
      (j) other loans
  (7) Trade credit
  (8) Proprietors' net investment in noncorporate business
  (9) Miscellaneous financial transactions.

In addition, private capital expenditures on consumer durable goods, non-farm residential construction, plant and equipment, and change in inventories are covered.

This series of statistics has particular relevance to this study. It comes the closest of any of the major series to providing complete aggregate information about the flow of funds through each of the categories open to the consumer for saving, as well as providing a balance sheet of financial asset holdings for the consumer sector. However, it has one of the same limitations of the other series in that the consumer sector includes nonprofit organizations such as foundations, private schools, unions, and so on. This means the statistics are somewhat inflated for use as indexes of consumer saving. In addition, the series cannot be used to study the portfolio composition or distributions of consumers.

Survey of Consumer Finances

Since 1946 annual studies of consumers' assets, debts, incomes, and financial attitudes have been carried out by the Survey Research Center of the University of Michigan. The Survey of Consumer Finances (SCF)[9] is the most notable attempt to use the survey technique to provide a continuous series of disaggregative statistics on consumers' financial behavior. From 1946 to 1959 the studies were sponsored by the Board of Governors of the Federal Reserve System and the results were regularly published in the *Federal Reserve Bulletin*. The 1960, 1961, and 1962

---

[9] Hereafter the Survey of Consumer Finances will be abbreviated to SCF.

Surveys were privately financed, and the results were published as monographs by the Survey Research Center.

Approximately 3,000 households are selected each year by probability sampling methods. The sample of households is drawn from throughout the United States (excluding Alaska and Hawaii) but does not include residents of institutions or military reservations. The coverage of assets has varied somewhat from study to study; however, consistent emphasis has been placed on obtaining estimates of the ownership and value of housing, consumer durables, liquid assets (deposits in banks, savings and loan associations, and credit unions, and United States government savings bonds), and selected other financial assets such as publicly traded stock and insurance.

Chapter 7 of the *1960 Survey* has particular relevance to this study.[10] Although the major emphasis is on description, some analysis of patterns of assets held by consumers and of portfolios subject to loss by inflation was undertaken in this section. This type of analysis is similar in some respects to the two divisions of the analysis in this monograph. However, the assets covered and the emphasis of the analysis is considerably different.

Patterns of asset holdings were studied in the following five asset categories: (1) liquid assets; (2) publicly traded common and preferred corporate stock; (3) equity in owner-occupied houses and farms; (4) other real estate; and (5) interest in unincorporated businesses. The major emphasis was placed on those consumer units who have at least $10,000 invested in at least one of the asset types.[11]

In Part Two of this study, emphasis is on the ownership of each asset, regardless of the amount held in the asset. And in addition to the assets considered in the *1960 Survey*, the ownership of life insurance, pension plans, loans lent, corporate and other bonds, marketable government securities, shares in mutual funds and investment clubs, and closely held corporate stocks are considered. However, the results of the *1960 Survey* and the correlation results obtained here for amounts held in various assets appear to be compatible, i.e., there is a lack of close correlation between amounts held in assets.[12]

The section of the *1960 Survey* dealing with portfolios subject to losses by inflation roughly corresponds to some of the analysis in Part Three of this study. In the SCF, portfolios which exceeded $5,000 in total assets were divided into three groups according to the relationship of liquid assets to corporate stock and real estate other than owner-occupied houses and farms. The three categories are portfolios in which liquid assets are

---

[10] Survey Research Center, *op. cit.*, pp. 111-48.
[11] *Ibid.*, p. 116.
[12] *Ibid.*, and page 45 of this study.

(1) substantially less than amounts held in stocks and real estate; (2) approximately the same as amounts held in stocks and real estate; and (3) substantially greater than amounts held in stock and real estate. The first category is called "inflation proof," the second "intermediate," and the third "non-inflation proof."[13]

The results of the analysis showed that there are more young people than old people with "inflation proof" portfolios and there are no income differences between the "intermediate" and the "non-inflation" strata. However, there are more high-income people in the "inflation proof" group than in the other categories.[14]

The introduction of unincorporated businesses into the analysis did not materially change the results. However, the ownership of owner-occupied homes is more frequent in the "non-inflation proof" group than in the "inflation proof" group. This indicates "that a very substantial part of those investors who have larger amounts in liquid assets than in corporate stock and other real estate are partly or entirely protected against inflation by investment in their own homes."[15]

No multivariate analysis was carried out to get a better explanation of the nature or the degree of the influence of the variables when all were considered at the same time.

The relationship of the foregoing analysis to Part Three is readily apparent. In Part Three the emphasis is on explaining the fixed- versus variable-dollar composition of the total portfolio. The "inflation proof" criterion of the SCF roughly corresponds to one set of the measures of fixed- versus variable-dollar composition used here. However, the asset coverage in this study is considerably broader and multivariate analysis was used throughout. In spite of the difference in asset coverage and the fact that the SCF related two types of assets to each other using broad class intervals for dollar amounts whereas here the actual ratio of the dollar amounts of variable-dollar assets to total assets was used, the result of the exclusion of home ownership produced similar results in both studies. For example, in this study when the equity in homes is included, most of the portfolios have over 60 percent of the total in variable-dollar assets (inflation proof) and if the home is excluded most of the portfolios have less than 40 percent of the total in fixed-dollar assets (non-inflation proof).

Major Historical Studies

Two historical studies of saving stand out as excellent sources of information about aggregate saving over substantial periods of time. These

---

[13] *Ibid.,* p. 117.
[14] *Ibid.,* p. 118.
[15] *Ibid.,* p. 119.

are Friend and Natrella's *Individuals' Saving* (mentioned earlier) and Goldsmith's *A Study of Saving in the United States.*[16]

Individuals' Saving

Friend and Natrella extended the SEC series "saving by individuals" back to the years 1929 to 1932 and presented in one source the total series from 1929 to 1952. In Part One of the volume the emphasis is on relating major bodies of saving data to various theories of saving. Part Two is devoted to a detailed analysis of the methodology used by the SEC in compiling their estimates of saving by individuals.

A Study of Saving in the United States

Goldsmith's *Study* is undoubtedly the most comprehensive compendium of aggregate statistics on saving ever compiled. It covers aggregate national saving and the saving of nonfarm households, farmers, unincorporated businesses, corporations, the federal government, state governments, and local governments for the years 1897 to 1949.

Volume 1 gives a summary of the findings of the study concerning trends and cyclical fluctuations in national saving by the various sectors and by forms of saving. Volume 2 covers aspects of the methodology employed in deriving the series and the relation of the estimates to other available data on saving. Volume 3 is a collection of special studies dealing with national wealth and national balance sheets; family saving; patterns of estate tax wealth; experiments with the saving function; estimates of national product, national income, and personal income; and an analysis of the value and distribution of the nonoperating assets of private, nonfinancial, nonprofit institutions.

The study of "The Pattern of Estate Tax Wealth" by Horst Mendershausen is particularly applicable to this analysis. The study is an attempt to "project the distribution of wealth among decedents into the entire population."[17] The method involves utilization of federal estate tax data and an "estate-multiplier" to compensate for the difference in age distribution between the decedents and the living. Although the data are applicable to less than 1 percent of the total population, it should be emphasized that this 1 percent is the wealthiest group in our society and they own the majority of such assets as stocks, bonds, and mortgages. The study covers the years from 1923 to 1947.

Of particular interest is the analysis of the composition of gross

---

[16] Raymond Goldsmith, *A Study of Saving in the United States,* Vols. 1, 2, and 3 (Princeton: Princeton University Press, 1955). Volume 3 is co-authored by Goldsmith, Dorothy S. Brady, and Horst Mendershausen and was published in 1956.

[17] Goldsmith, Brady, and Mendershausen, *op. cit.,* p. 279.

estates by type of property and by the size and composition of estates.[18] In the section on the composition of gross estates by type of property, the percentage of the total estate held in each of the following asset categories is traced through years 1922 to 1946: real estate, federal government bonds, state and municipal bonds, corporate bonds, corporate stock, cash, mortgages and notes, insurance, interest in unincorporated businesses, and other intangible property. During this period real estate decreased in relative importance (from 24.7 percent to 18.1 percent of the gross estate) and intangible property increased in relative importance (from 75.3 percent to 80.8 percent of the gross estate). Insurance, corrected for the difference between the cash value and estate settlement value, stayed at about 7 percent of the gross estate from about 1942 on.[19]

In the section relating size of the gross estate to the composition of the estate, eight class intervals are used, the smallest being under $100,000 and the largest being $5,000,000 and over in gross estate. In general, the author found

a notable constancy in the typical composition of estates of similar dollar value. Compared with a small net estate, a large one shows *relatively* less real estate, mortgages, notes, cash, insurance, interest in unincorporated business, and indebtedness. It shows *relatively* more stocks and government bonds, particularly state and municipal bonds, but little more, or even less corporate bonds.[20]

In 1946 the aggregate proportion of the gross estate held in cash, mortgages and notes, and other intangibles (the categories which roughly correspond to fixed-dollar assets) decreased relatively as the size of the gross estate increased. The proportions for the lowest category ("under $100,000") and the highest category ("$5,000,000 and over") were 18.8 percent and 7.1 percent, respectively.[21] Comparable results are found in this study for portfolio composition in 1960, i.e., size of the total portfolio varies inversely with the proportion of the total portfolio held in fixed-dollar assets.

In another section of the study a series of multiple correlations were carried out to explain the variation in the amounts held in federal government bonds, state and municipal bonds, insurance, and unincorporated business.[22] The independent variables used were value of the gross estate and age of the decedent. The coefficients of multiple correlation ranged from .89 for federal government bonds to .69 for unincorporated business. The only relation in which age contributed significantly was unincorporated business and in this function the regression coefficient for age was

[18] *Ibid.*, pp. 308-19 and 323-32.
[19] *Ibid.*, pp. 310-11.
[20] *Ibid.*, p. 323.
[21] *Ibid.*, p. 328.
[22] *Ibid.*, p. 366.

negative.[23] No correlations explaining portfolio composition were carried out.

Analytical Studies of Saving in General

The emphasis of this section is on studies of consumer savings behavior which are relevant to the problem of portfolio composition. Since the body of data collected in the annual SCF is the major source of data amenable to this type of analysis, most of the studies are based on this source.

Investment by Individuals

Data collected in the 1946-49 SCFs and from a sample of 746 customers of investment banking firms were used by Butters, Thompson, and Bollinger to study the effect of taxation on investment behavior.[24] Although portfolio composition was not the primary concern of the inquiry, one part of the investigation is particularly relevant.

An analysis of various assets as a percentage of total wealth, somewhat similar to that presented by Mendershausen, shows that as total wealth increases from under $25,000 to over $1,000,000 the percentage of total assets held in liquid assets decreases from 35 percent to 10 percent.[25] And as income increases from under $7,500 to over $50,000, the percentage of the sample having 0-19 percent of their total assets in liquid assets increases from 45 percent to 74 percent, whereas the percentage having over 60 percent of their total assets in liquid assets decreases from 11 percent to 1 percent.[26]

Similar results were found here. As pointed out earlier, total assets appear to be the most important factor in determining the proportion of the total portfolio which is held in liquid, fixed-dollar assets.

Analysis of Liquid Asset Ownership

A second study utilizing Survey of Consumer Finances data is that done by Kreinin on liquid asset ownership.[27] This investigation was carried out using 2,854 nonfarm spending units covered in the 1957 SCF. Kreinin utilized the analysis of variance technique to determine the factors which were associated with the ownership and amount held in liquid assets. He found that income, education, occupation, and geographic region were significant at the .01 probability level in explaining

---

[23] *Ibid.*

[24] J. K. Butters, L. D. Thompson, and L. L. Bollinger, *Investment by Individuals* (Boston: Harvard University Press, 1953).

[25] *Ibid.*, pp. 299-315.

[26] *Ibid.*, pp. 300 and 303.

[27] Mordechai E. Kreinin, "Analysis of Liquid Asset Ownership," *Review of Economics and Statistics*, Vol. 43, No. 1 (February, 1961), pp. 76-80.

the ownership of liquid assets.[28] Income, occupation, age, and geographic region were also found to be significant in the analysis of amounts held in liquid assets. However, the interactions of these factors, and education as a separate variable were not significant in the analysis of the amounts held in liquid assets.[29]

The most interesting part of Kreinin's research, from the perspective of this study, is the analysis of the composition of asset holdings. In this section financial assets were divided into liquid assets and stocks and bonds. Here Kreinin found that four-fifths of all owners of financial assets own only liquid assets, and for the remaining fifth "the question of whether they hold mostly variable money value assets is in the large part a matter of attitude and environment." Kreinin goes on to say,

Spending units who prefer to remain liquid hold a higher proportion of their financial assets in the form of liquid assets. The higher the proportion thus held, the larger the amount of liquid assets owned compared to what would be expected on the basis of the spending units' socioeconomic characteristics. Conversely, people who prefer variable money assets tend to hold large proportions of their financial assets in stock. And the larger the proportion so held, the smaller the amount of liquid assets owned as compared to what is expected on the basis of socioeconomic variables.[30]

Kreinin made no attempt to explain why people prefer to remain liquid or why they prefer to hold variable money assets. However, he did point out that an earlier study of stock ownership showed that attitudes about investment preference and security-mindedness (conservativeness) were significantly associated with the type of assets owned.[31] No mention is made in the study of motives for saving and the influence motives might have on the composition of portfolios. Nor is an attempt made to isolate the "environmental" factors which may explain this type of variation.

Although Kreinin's inquiry is similar in some respects to the second part of this analysis, the emphasis here is on explaining the variation in the ratio of variable-dollar assets to total assets, rather than on using this ratio to explain the ownership of liquid assets. In addition, the asset coverage here is broader and psychological factors such as motives for saving, expectations, and personality characteristics are brought into the model.

Propensities to Hold Liquid Assets

The third study referred to earlier was done by Guthrie and deals with "Consumers' Propensities to Hold Liquid Assets."[32] Data collected in the

---

[28] *Ibid.*, p. 76.

[29] *Ibid.*, p. 77.

[30] *Ibid.*, p. 79.

[31] *Ibid.*

[32] Harold W. Guthrie, "Consumers' Propensities to Hold Liquid Assets," *Journal of the American Statistical Association,* Vol. 55, No. 291 (September, 1960), pp. 469-90.

1947-53 SCFs were utilized in an attempt to explain the variation in ratios of liquid assets to total annual income (LA ratio) for different strata of spending units. The sample was first stratified into single-person and multiple-person spending units. Then, each of these strata was subdivided according to whether it was in a high income, temporarily low income, or permanently low income group.[33]

In the cross-section analysis of 1953 data, Guthrie specified a regression model for each of these groups and made the LA ratio a function of the age of the head of the spending unit, number of persons in the spending unit, the spending unit's income decile, and home ownership. The results of this analysis are particularly relevant to this study. For example, age was found to have a significant positive relation to the LA ratio in all cases except single-person spending units with temporarily low income; size of spending unit was significant and negative in all income groups; income decile was significant and negative only for single-person units in the temporarily low and permanently low income strata; and home ownership was significant and negative for only the single-person high-income stratum.[34]

One of the conclusions Guthrie draws is that the absence of a substitution effect between liquid assets and equity in homes suggests that "consumers do not shift between asset forms while maintaining some normative level of security in total wealth. Rather it is possible that each form of asset has a desired normal level and there is no 'portfolio problem.' "[35]

Although the asset coverage and the methodology employed is somewhat different, the results are not incompatible with the results presented here. For example, in Part Two, an absence of a substitution effect among assets was found for nearly all assets; and in Part Three, each time an age variable was significant it was positively related to fixed-dollar assets (nearly the same as the liquid dollar classification) and each time income was significant it was negatively related to fixed-dollar assets. The differences in the dependent variables and methodology preclude meaningful comparisons of the size of the regression coefficients and other aspects of the analysis.

British Savings Studies

A series of studies of consumer savings patterned after the SCFs were carried out in Great Britain in 1952-54. The results are reported in Lydall's *British Incomes and Savings*.[36] Although the asset coverage is

---

[33] *Ibid.*, pp. 472-73.
[34] *Ibid.*, p. 476.
[35] *Ibid.*, p. 478.
[36] Harold F. Lydall, *British Incomes and Savings* (Oxford: Basil Blackwell, 1955).

limited and the data related to Great Britain rather than to the United States, the research is relevant to this sudy because it is one of the few attempts to describe combinations of assets owned by consumers.[37] However, the approach is mainly descriptive and no mention is made of the effect of interaction between assets on asset ownership.

Studies of Portfolio Components

Studies of the demand for or ownership distributions of selected assets available to consumers as investment and saving alternatives are constantly being made by business enterprises and trade associations dealing in these assets. Unfortunately, most of this literature is not available to the public. Of the reports which are available to the general public, perhaps the greatest number deal with the demand for durable goods and secondarily with the influence of liquid assets on consumption goods and durable goods. These analyses are, of course, relevant to the general subject of this monograph. However, since data which would allow comparison with studies of durable goods were not available for this study, this literature is not reviewed here.[38]

Of the inquiries dealing with other components of consumer savings such as life insurance, stocks, and savings and loan shares, the following are particularly applicable to this analysis.

Factors Associated with Stock Ownership

In Kreinin's study of the factors associated with stock ownership, an analysis of variance revealed that the following four factors were associated with the dependent variable — education, income, liquid assets, and occupation.[39] Only income and liquid assets were found to be significantly related to the amount of stocks owned.[40]

In an analysis of the residuals, Kreinin found

(1) "security minded" spending units owned less stock than did "accomplishment minded" spending units;

(2) no apparent relation between stock ownership and price expectations;

---

[37] *Ibid.*, pp. 61-84.

[38] For examples of this work, see George Katona, *Psychological Analysis of Consumer Behavior* (New York: McGraw-Hill, 1951); selected articles in Lawrence Klein, *Contributions of Survey Methods to Economics* (New York: Columbia University Press, 1954); Robert Ferber, "Factors Influencing Durable Goods Purchases," in Lincoln Clark, ed., *Consumer Behavior*, Vol. 2 (New York: New York University Press, 1955), pp. 75-112; and James Morgan, "Consumer Investment Expenditures," *American Economic Review*, Vol. 48, No. 4 (December, 1958), pp. 874-902.

[39] Mordechai E. Kreinin, "Factors Associated with Stock Ownership," *Review of Economics and Statistics*, Vol. 41, No. 1 (February, 1959), pp. 12-23.

[40] *Ibid.*, p. 17.

(3) a positive relation between willingness to take risks and stock and real estate ownership rates and amounts; and

(4) a positive relationship between optimistic people and stock ownership.[41]

Kreinin concludes that socioeconomic factors provide only a partial explanation of stock ownership, and other variables such as psychological factors must be brought into the analysis.[42]

Although the dependent variable in Kreinin's analysis and in this study are slightly different, stocks represent a large part of the variable-dollar segment of portfolios (particularly of large portfolios) and Kreinin's results are relevant here. Similar results were found in both studies for the influence of socioeconomic variables and psychological variables, e.g.,

(1) socioeconomic variables do not explain the greater part of the variance of the dependent variables in either case,

(2) price expectations, contrary to a priori reasoning, are not significantly related to the dependent variables, and

(3) both analyses point to the importance of other psychological variables.

Other, more descriptive studies of stock ownership have been carried out under the auspices of the New York Stock Exchange.[43]

Pension Plans and Aggregate Saving

A second study of portfolio components deals with the effect of pension plan coverage on saving. It is based on information collected from 15,873 households who are customers of Consumers Union (a national products testing organization).[44]

Cagan's major emphasis is on the influence of pension plan coverage on aggregate saving, but one section of the analysis is devoted to the effect of pension plan coverage on equity in real estate, equity in insurance and annuities, cash and securities, and non-mortgage debt. An analysis of variance showed that "in addition to the absence of substitution of pension contributions from total other saving . . . substitution is also absent from each component of other saving. . . ."[45]

These results clearly support those found in Part Two where the data

---

[41] *Ibid.*, pp. 19-20.

[42] *Ibid.*, p. 21.

[43] See Lewis H. Kimmel, *Share Ownership in the United States* (Washington: Brookings, 1952); New York Stock Exchange, *Who Owns American Business: 1956 Census of Shareowners* (New York: New York Stock Exchange, 1957); and New York Stock Exchange, *Share Ownership in America: 1959* (New York: New York Stock Exchange, 1960).

[44] Phillip Cagan, "Pension Plans and Aggregate Savings" (Unpublished manuscript, Brown University, 1961).

[45] *Ibid.*, pp. 3-19.

indicate that there is an absence of interaction between assets ownership as well as between amounts held in various assets.

Consumer Savings Project

The work of the Consumer Savings Project is particularly relevant to this investigation since all of the empirical data used here were collected in the course of the studies carried out by the Project. The use of the Consumer Savings Project data makes it possible to eliminate, to a large extent, a common disadvantage of all of the analyses cited earlier, i.e., all of the latter studies were based on data which are known to be biased toward underestimation of asset ownership and amounts held in assets. For example, it has been estimated that estimates of aggregate liquid assets based on SCF data understate actual total liquid assets by about one-third.[46]

This problem of understatement of aggregate savings encountered by most, if not all, surveys on consumer savings and the recognition of the need for better statistics fostered the sponsorship of the Consumer Savings Project in 1957 by the Inter-University Committee for Research on Consumer Behavior.[47]

The primary objective of the Consumer Savings Project was to develop and test the methodology necessary to obtain accurate and reliable data on consumers' saving and financial positions. The work of this project, utilizing the panel technique (repeated reinterviewing of the same people),[48] has provided a body of data which is unique. Through the cooperation of financial institutions it was possible to make corrections for known biases in consumer reports of ownership and amounts held in certain assets,[49] and thus obtain a more accurate body of data.

---

[46] See Subcommittee, *op. cit.,* pp. 278-87; and John B. Lansing and Harold F. Lydall, "A Comparison of the Distribution of Personal Income and Wealth in the United States and Great Britain," *American Economic Review,* Vol. 49, No. 1 (March, 1959), p. 58.

[47] The Inter-University Committee consists of the following seven experts in various fields from six institutions: Guy Orcutt, University of Wisconsin; Lincoln Clark, New York University; Robert Ferber, University of Illinois; Raymond Goldsmith, Yale University; George Katona, Theodore Newcomb, University of Michigan; and James Tobin, Yale University.

[48] Robert Ferber, *Collecting Financial Data by Consumer Panel Techniques* (Urbana: University of Illinois, Bureau of Economic and Business Research, 1959); John B. Lansing, Gerald P. Ginsburg, and Kaisa Braaten, *An Investigation of Response Error* (Urbana: University of Illinois, Bureau of Economic and Business Research, 1961).

[49] A single interview study in which some forms of saving were validated was made in Holland. See W. Horn, "Reliability Survey, A Survey on the Reliability of Responses to an Interview Survey," *Het PTT-bedrijf,* Vol. 10, No. 3 (October, 1960).

Scope

Period Covered

This study represents a static, cross-section analysis of the portfolios of consumer savings units (SUs)[50] at one point in time — early spring of 1960. The data were collected over approximately five weeks — from late January to early March of 1960.

Population Covered

The sample used is not representative of the population at large. It was drawn from SUs in two major metropolitan areas and has a strong upper-income and high-asset-ownership bias. There is no representation from nonurban dwellers and much less than proportional representation of low-income groups. Hence the results, particularly those relating to proportions owning certain assets, should not be construed as being representative of the general population of the United States.

Holdings Covered

The scope of asset and debt coverage, though broad, is not all inclusive. The assets included are checking accounts, savings accounts in commercial banks, savings and loan shares, credit union shares, postal savings, savings-type life insurance, pension plans, annuities, government savings bonds, marketable government securities, loans and mortgages lent, corporate stocks, mutual fund shares, shares in investment clubs, brokerage accounts, corporate bonds, municipal and other bonds, personal trusts, owner-occupied homes, other real estate, and businesses (both incorporated and unincorporated). The only form of debt treated separately is non-mortgage debt of more than 30 days' duration. Mortgages on real estate have been deducted from the gross value of the real estate.

The major omissions are cash, consumer durable goods, and debt which was expected to be paid off within 30 days from the date of the interview. In addition, although the ownership of life insurance and pension plans are covered, the cash value of these two assets is not included. While most consumers know the face value of their life insurance policies and probable monthly retirement benefits of their pension plans, very few know the present cash value of these assets. Hence, these amounts have been omitted from the aggregate amount of savings.

---

[50] Hereafter savings unit will be abbreviated to SU. An SU is defined as one or more persons living in the same dwelling, pooling half or more of their income and savings. A dwelling unit may therefore have more than one SU.

Methodology
Description of the Sample

The entire sample was drawn using restricted random selection methods. However, there was a difference in sample design in the two cities covered. One segment of the sample was drawn, utilizing census tract information, from the total population of the city. There was substantial over-sampling of the upper-income census tracts. The second segment of the sample was drawn from lists of known owners of certain assets. Data utilized in this study were collected on the fifth reinterview (approximately 15 months after the first interview) in one city and on the third reinterview (approximately 9 months after the first interview) in the second city. The 405 SUs included in this study represent 77 percent of the original number of SUs covered on the first interview in both cities.[51] The sample designs resulted in a sample which obviously does not represent a cross section of all urban families. For example, of the 384 SUs who gave income figures, 34.4 percent had more than $10,000 income in 1959; 9.9 percent had more than $25,000; and only 22.4 percent had less than $5,000 total income in 1959. The high-income bias and the sample design in the second city also means that the rate of asset ownership of the sample is considerably higher than that of the total population.

The data were collected by personal interviews utilizing a structured questionnaire.[52]

Plan of the Analysis and Techniques Employed

Before any analysis of the data was undertaken a "best estimate" of the ownership and amount held in the asset was made. The information obtained from financial institutions was utilized in the derivation of the best estimate. (The procedure is outlined in Appendix A.) On those assets for which validating information was not available, a consistency check of all of the data reported on earlier waves was made.

The analysis of portfolio composition is carried out in two parts — (1) the asset composition of portfolios and (2) the fixed- versus variable-dollar composition of the portfolio. Although the fixed- and variable-dollar categories in Part Three are aggregates of the individual assets analyzed in Part Two, the basic questions asked in each part are different. Consequently, the analysis and the explanation of the results are handled separately for each part.

---

[51] No corrections have been made for possible biases which may be caused by panel mortality.

[52] A structured questionnaire is one in which all questions are recorded in a certain order on the form and are worded as they are to be asked by the interviewer.

In Part Two the emphasis is on the actual combinations of holdings owned and on the interaction between holdings. The basic questions asked are

(1) What are the actual portfolios owned?

(2) What is the effect of the ownership of one holding or combination of holdings on ownership of another holding or combination of holdings?

To answer these questions the proportions of the sample owning all possible combinations of two holdings (assets or debt), and selected combinations of holdings from three at a time to nine at a time are computed for the total sample and for strata within the sample. These ownership rates (proportions) are then compared with the corresponding ownership rates which would be expected if the holdings were independent of each other. The differences between the actual and the expected proportions are then tested for statistical and operational significance. In addition, the absolute differences are converted to relative differences and their predictive usefulness is investigated.

In Chapter III the results of the analysis carried out in Chapter II are recast in a probability framework relating the ownership of assets to the motives for holding assets. And last, the results of the analysis and the whole problem of portfolio selection are restated in the framework of a generally accepted theory of behavior.

In Part Three the emphasis is on the percentage of the total dollar value of the portfolio which is held in variable-dollar assets. The basic question asked is, What factors explain the fixed- versus variable-dollar composition of consumer savings portfolios and what is the nature of their influence?

In order to answer this question, the proportion of the portfolio held in variable-dollar assets is made a function of various socioeconomic and psychological variables in several multiple regression functions. Two separate measures of the variable-dollar composition of portfolios are used as dependent variables in the analyses. The first is a measure of the composition of the total portfolio — the ratio of total variable-dollar assets to total assets. The second is a measure of the composition of that part of the portfolio which the SU can exercise considerable discretion in managing. The dependent variable for the composition of the discretionary portfolio is found by computing the ratio of variable-dollar assets, exclusive of the equity in owner-occupied homes, to total assets, exclusive of the equity in owner-occupied homes and balances in checking accounts.

Valuation and Consolidation of Holdings

The best estimate of the cash value of each asset on the date of the interview was made by utilizing validation information and all data reported by the SU on earlier waves. The valuation procedure and groupings of assets are outlined below.

Fixed-dollar Assets

Savings accounts. All savings accounts and certificates in commercial banks, mutual savings banks, postal savings, shares in savings and loan associations, shares in credit unions; valued at balance on date of interview.

Checking accounts. All accounts in commercial banks subject to checking privileges; valued at balance on date of interview.

Government savings bonds. All non-marketable government bonds sold to individuals either at a discount, or at face value; valued at redemption value at date of interview. (The vast majority are Series E bonds.)

Loans and mortgages lent. All personal loans, mortgages, or contracts to individuals or institutions other than those in or controlled by the SU; valued at balance outstanding on the date of interview.

Annuities. All annuities, exempt of life insurance clauses; valued at the SU's equity (payments plus accrued interest).

Life insurance. All savings-type life insurance policies, i.e., policies which build up cash value for the holder; valued at face value at date of interview. Term, accident, and group policies are omitted.

Variable-dollar Assets

Stocks. Common stocks, preferred stocks, shares in investment companies, shares in investment clubs, and brokerage accounts; valued at closing market price on February 1, 1960. Quotations on stocks which were not listed on the organized exchanges or traded over the counter were obtained from a stock broker. In a few cases where the broker was unable to secure a quotation the SU's estimate of the value of the stock was taken as the best estimate. (Stock in a business controlled by the SU is listed under business.)

Bonds. Corporate, municipal, marketable government securities, and all other bonds such as church bonds; valued at closing market price on February 1, 1960, broker's quotation, or SU's estimate of present market price.

Owner-occupied home. The residence which the SU occupies; valued at the SU's equity, i.e., the current market price, less any outstanding mortgages.

Other real estate. All real estate owned by the SU, other than the home in which they reside; valued at the SU's equity, i.e., the current market price less outstanding mortgages.

Business. Any business incorporated or unincorporated in which the SU exercises control over the operations of the business; valued at the SU's estimate of the net asset value of the business.

PART TWO

COMBINATIONS OF HOLDINGS

II. THE ASSET COMPOSITION OF PORTFOLIOS

In the analysis of the asset composition of the total portfolio all combinations of 13 holdings — 12 assets and debt — are considered.[53] The assets included are checking accounts, savings accounts, life insurance, pension plans, government savings bonds, other bonds, annuities, loans lent, stocks, business, owner-occupied home, and other real estate. The only debt considered is non-mortgage debt of more than 30 days' duration.

The Problem

Table 1 gives the percentage ownership distribution of each of the 13 holdings. It is obvious from Table 1 that certain assets such as owner-occupied homes, checking accounts, life insurance, and savings accounts must appear in nearly all of the portfolios. A priori reasoning leads one to expect a typical portfolio consisting of these assets, or these and one or two other assets, for large numbers of SUs with similar socioeconomic characteristics. However, examination of the actual combinations (portfolios) of holdings owned shows that this is not the case. Without an aggregate classification system, such as the fixed- versus variable-dollar one, there are no "typical" portfolios for large segments of the sample. The extreme heterogeneity of portfolios is illustrated by the fact that most of the combinations are held by only one or two SUs. (The maximum dispersion would be found if every SU owned a different combination of assets.) There are 203 different portfolios owned by the 384 SUs who gave income information and the largest number of SUs owning the same portfolio is 17.

Development of the Independence Hypothesis

Surprisingly, this result can be predicted if one assumes that the holdings are independent. In other words, if the ownership of one asset or debt does not influence the probability of ownership of a second, i.e., there is no interaction, then the expected proportion (or number of

[53] The "asset composition of portfolios" is to some extent a misnomer, since one type of debt is included in the analysis. However, the major emphasis of the analysis is on the interaction of assets.

27

TABLE 1. PERCENTAGE OWNERSHIP DISTRIBUTION
OF 13 HOLDINGS, FOR 384 SAVINGS UNITS

Assets	Percentage
Life insurance...	89.6
Own home..	84.6
Other real estate.......................................	23.4
Checking account.......................................	85.9
Pension plan...	46.4
Savings account..	89.6
Government savings bonds...............................	53.9
Other bonds...	10.7
Stocks..	46.9
Loans lent...	14.8
Business..	19.3
Annuities...	7.0
Debt...	29.7

SUs) owning any combination of holdings can be found by multiplying
the proportions owning each of the holdings in the combination. If this
product is multiplied by the product of the complements to the proportions of the holdings not included in the given combination, the final
product is the expected proportion owning exactly the given combination.
Stated symbolically the proposition is as follows: let

$H_1, H_2, \ldots, H_n$ = total number of holdings possible,

C = any combination of the holdings (portfolio),

$\overline{C}$ = all holdings not in C,

H' = any single holding in C, where there are m holdings in C and
$m \leq n$, and

H'' = any single holding in $\overline{C}$.

The expected proportion owning any combination (portfolio) C,
under an assumption of independence is

(2.1) $$P(C) = P(H')_1 P(H')_2, \ldots, P(H')_m.$$

And the expected proportion owning exactly C and no other holding is

(2.2) $$P(C) P(\overline{C}) = P(H')_1 P(H')_2 \ldots P(H')_m [1 - P(H'')_{m+1}]$$
$$[1 - P(H'')_{m+2}] \ldots [1 - P(H'')_n].$$

For example, the six assets in the modal portfolio mentioned above
are pension plans, life insurance, checking accounts, savings accounts,
government bonds, and homes. If proportions owning each of the six
listed assets are multiplied, the product or expected proportion of the
sample owning the combination is .146, or 14.6 percent.

If the complements to the proportions owning the seven holdings
not included in the modal portfolio are multiplied, the product is .163,

or 16.3 percent. Thus, the expected proportion owning exactly the modal portfolio is .146 × .163 = .024, or 2.4 percent. The actual percentage of the sample owning the modal portfolio is 4.4 percent. The difference of 2 percent is remarkably small when one considers that the actual proportion of the samples owning the model portfolio could be any place between 0 and 46.4 percent (see equations 2.4 and 2.5). Thus, from an operational point of view, the results may be significant. Similar results found for many different portfolios strongly indicate that the ownership of holdings may be independent. That is, the ownership of one holding, or combination of holdings, does not influence the probability of ownership of another holding, or combination of holdings. This independence hypothesis can be stated as a null hypothesis and tested for statistical as well as operational significance.

For example, in the case of four holdings, let

$P(H_1)$ = the proportion owning holding one,
$P(H_2)$ = the proportion owning holding two,
$P(H_3)$ = the proportion owning holding three,
$P(H_4)$ = the proportion owning holding four,
$P(H_1 H_2 H_3 H_4) = A$ = the proportion owning holdings one to four, and
$P(H_1)\ P(H_2)\ P(H_3)\ P(H_4) = E$ = the expected proportion of the sample owning holdings one to four.

Then, the independence (null) hypothesis to be tested is [54]

(2.3) $$A - E = d = O.$$

Implications of the Independence Hypothesis

This hypothesis, if valid, may have many important implications. First, it means that in specification of the factors influencing the demand for a given asset, the interaction of that asset with other assets can be disregarded. Once the proportions owning the individual assets are known, the actual portfolios can be predicted by multiplying the independent proportions. It also means that in the specification of the factors influencing the composition of the total portfolio, the substitutability or complementarity of assets need not be considered.

Moreover, the independence hypothesis may provide financial institutions with a reliable means of predicting the proportion of their cus-

---

[54] Since the sampling distribution of d is not known, a reasonable approximation would appear to be the standard T test utilizing A, E, and σ_A. Throughout the remainder of Part Two the emphasis will be on determining the validity of the independence hypothesis in predicting the proportion of the sample owning *at least* the holdings specified; consequently, the prime and double prime notation is dropped. Thus, in this example, additional holdings besides H_1 and H_2 may or may not be owned.

tomers, or potential customers, who own given combinations of assets. Or it may be used to predict what proportions of a population do *not* own specified combinations of assets. Information of this type is invaluable to financial institutions in the formulation of their marketing policy and action.

Perhaps the most important aspect of independence is that it may provide insights, otherwise unobtainable, into the way people act — insights into the way they select portfolios and why.

Since the problem of the asset composition of portfolios becomes a problem of individual assets if independence holds, the major emphasis of this section is on determining the operational and statistical significance of the independence hypothesis.

Tests of Independence

Combinations of Two Holdings

Total Sample

Table 2 gives the percentage of the sample owning all possible combinations of two assets, or of one asset and debt. The main diagonal from the upper left to the lower right gives the percentage of the sample owning the asset listed in that row and column. The cells to the left of the diagonal give the percentage of the sample owning the combination listed. The cells to the right of the diagonal give the value of d (the deviation) for each of the 78 combinations. For example, 89.6 percent of the SUs own life insurance, 53.9 percent own government bonds, and 48.2 percent of the SUs own both life insurance and government bonds. The deviation (d) between the actual percentage owning life insurance and government bonds and the expected percentage is $-.1$ percent.

Immediately striking is the large number of cells with very small values of d. Forty-one of the 78 deviations are less than 1 percentage point and in three cases A equals E. In only eight of the 78 cases are the deviations statistically significant at the .05 level. Out of this number of tests and at this confidence level, one would expect approximately three tests to be significant, owing to chance alone.

Additional information about independence can be obtained from examination of the signs of d and the pattern of their occurrence. If the assets and debts are actually independent there should be approximately as many minus signs as plus signs for each of the assets and the sum of the deviations should be approximately equal to zero. Table 2 shows that this is clearly not the case. There are twice as many positive as negative deviations and there are distinct patterns to their occurrence.

Combinations of debt and assets yield three plus signs and seven

TABLE 2. PERCENTAGE OF SAMPLE OWNING EACH HOLDING, COMBINATIONS OF TWO HOLDINGS, AND DEVIATIONS[a] BETWEEN ACTUAL AND EXPECTED PERCENTAGES, FOR 384 SAVINGS UNITS

Holding	Holding												
	Life insurance	Own home	Other real estate	Checking account	Pension plan	Savings account	Government bonds	Other bonds	Stocks	Loans lent	Business	Annuities	Debt
Life insurance	*89.6*	+1.5	-.4	-.4	+.8	+.7	-.1	-.5	-.1	+.2	-.9	+.2	+2.0
Own home	77.3	*84.6*	+1.6	+2.0	+3.1	-1.3	+3.6	.0	+1.7	-1.3	+1.9	-.2	-.9
Other real estate	20.6	21.4	*23.4*	+2.8	-2.0	-.6	+.9	+1.1	+3.3	+.7	+1.0	-.8	-.7
Checking account	76.6	74.7	22.9	*85.9*	-1.1	+.1	+2.7	+1.0	+5.3[b]	+.6	+1.9	+.5	-1.3
Pension plan	42.4	42.4	8.9	38.8	*46.4*	+1.1	+4.2	-.1	+.3	+.1	-5.1[b]	+1.7	-1.6
Savings account	81.0	77.1	20.8	77.1	42.7	*89.6*	+1.2	-.2	-.1	+.4	-.2	+.2	-.8
Government bonds	48.2	49.2	13.5	49.0	29.2	49.5	*53.9*	+1.0	+5.2[b]	+.6	+.3	+2.0	-3.8[b]
Other bonds	9.1	9.1	3.6	10.2	4.9	9.4	6.8	*10.7*	+3.6[b]	.0	+2.6[b]	+.6	-.6
Stocks	41.9	41.4	14.3	45.6	22.1	41.9	30.5	8.6	*46.9*	+1.4	+2.9[b]	+2.2[b]	-1.1
Loans lent	13.5	11.2	4.2	13.3	7.0	13.8	8.6	1.6	8.3	*14.8*	+.2	+.3	++
Business	18.2	18.2	5.5	18.5	3.9	17.2	10.7	4.7	12.0	3.1	*19.3*	-.4	+.8
Annuities	6.5	5.7	.8	6.5	4.9	6.5	5.7	1.3	5.5	1.3	1.0	*7.0*	.0
Debt	28.6	24.2	6.2	24.2	12.2	25.8	12.2	2.6	12.8	4.7	6.5	2.1	*29.7*

a In percentage points.
b Statistically significant at the .05 level.

minus signs. The largest negative d is for debt and government bonds. The largest positive d is for debt and life insurance. This general finding supports a priori reasoning about the relation between the specific assets and debt. First, life insurance is an important source of this type of debt; therefore there should be a positive relation between the two. Second, because liquid assets such as government bonds can easily be used for the same purpose as debt, the number of SUs holding both is likely to be smaller than the expected number if they were actually independent. The striking result is that with a sample size of 384 there are not more combinations with large differences.

Five of the eight significant deviations involve stock ownership. These results indicate that there may be a positive relationship between stock and each of the following assets: checking accounts, government bonds, businesses, bonds, and annuities. The only negative signs involving stock ownership are found for life insurance and savings accounts. Thus, in the aggregate at least, the results indicate that stocks may be complementary to most assets except savings accounts and life insurance.

The signs of d for government bonds follow a pattern similar to that of stocks. The deviations for all combinations of government bonds and other assets, except life insurance, are positive. In view of this positive tendency, it is possible that a larger sample size would produce more tests in which d is significantly different from zero.

The business-pension plan case is the only combination of two assets having a significant negative value of d. It should be pointed out that this result may be caused by the nature of the two assets and not by their substitutability. This result may arise because company pension plans are established primarily for the employees and in many cases the owners are excluded from membership. Thus, the results of the tests are to be expected, i.e., that the expected proportion for business and pension plans is significantly larger than the actual proportion.

In general the results presented in Table 2 indicate that there is a slight complementarity between assets, particularly stock and government bonds, and a slight negative relation between assets and debt. However, these relations are not pronounced, and it appears that independence is not far from the actual case for most combinations.

Subgroups of the Sample

It may be that the independence hypothesis is valid on an aggregate level but breaks down when subgroups of the sample are tested. In order to test this possibility the sample has been divided into two strata — those with less than $25,000 and those with over $25,000 in total assets.

A priori, it may be reasoned that SUs with fewer funds are faced by a constraint which limits the number and type of assets they may practicably consider. For example, they have a need for emergency funds which are safe and liquid. In general, fixed-dollar assets meet these requirements better than do variable-dollar assets. In addition, variable-dollar assets are less divisible than fixed-dollar assets (e.g., most corporate bonds are sold in multiples of $1,000, but a very small amount can start a savings account). Hence, these SUs could be expected to concentrate their holdings in fixed-dollar assets, and within the fixed-dollar category, in specific assets. Thus, the proportions owning each of the fixed-dollar assets may be relatively high, but the proportions owning combinations of fixed-dollar assets which are good substitutes may be considerably below the independence estimate. For example, savings accounts and government bonds may be regarded as close substitutes on most dimensions. Both have their principal guaranteed by the federal government, are highly liquid, are convenient to acquire, and have comparable rates of return. Hence, the SU may be indifferent as to which is owned, but the ownership of both is unnecessary. On the other hand, most, if not all, SUs with limited funds who invest in variable-dollar assets such as stock could be expected to have fixed-dollar components in their portfolios. This would mean that the expected value of combinations of fixed- and variable-dollar assets would be considerably less than the actual value.

SUs with larger savings have more freedom in the selection of assets and should be better able to diversify their portfolios. This freedom of action, unless there are clear substitutes and complements in the minds of substantial numbers of individuals, would likely lead to independence estimates which are very close to the actual proportions.

Tables 3 and 4 give the proportions owning each of the assets, combinations of two, and the deviations of the expected value from the actual value for the 176 SUs who have less than $25,000 and the 146 SUs who have over $25,000 in total savings.[55]

The difference in ownership rates for the various assets is immediately apparent. Virtually all of the SUs with larger amounts of savings own their own homes and checking accounts, compared with about 75 percent of the SUs with smaller total savings. Also, substantially more of the larger portfolios contain stocks, government bonds, real estate, businesses, bonds, and annuities than do the smaller portfolios. The reverse situation is true for life insurance and debt, i.e., relatively more of the smaller portfolios contain these items than the larger portfolios. This indicates that there is a distinct difference in emphasis, similar to

---

[55] Combinations involving bonds and annuities have been omitted from Table 3 and combinations involving homes and checking accounts have been eliminated from Table 4. This was done because the range of the possible deviation is so small that it was impossible for the deviations to be statistically significant.

TABLE 3. PERCENTAGE OF SAMPLE OWNING EACH HOLDING, COMBINATIONS OF TWO HOLDINGS, AND DEVIATIONS[a] BETWEEN ACTUAL AND EXPECTED PERCENTAGES, FOR 176 SAVINGS UNITS WITH LESS THAN $25,000 IN TOTAL ASSETS[b]

Holding	Life insurance	Own home	Other real estate	Checking account	Pension plan	Savings account	Government bonds	Stocks	Loans lent	Business	Debt
						Holding					
Life insurance	92.6	+.5	+.8	-1.1	+.7	-1.2	-.8	+.6	-.8	-.6	+2.1
Own home	71.0	76.1	-.1	+.1	+1.4	-.5	+3.5	+1.6	+.4	+.7	+.6
Other real estate	10.2	7.4	10.2	+1.9	-2.2	-.7	-1.0	+.4	+1.0	-.2	+1.4
Checking account	69.9	58.5	9.7	76.7	-2.3	-.5	+.4	+4.3	+1.2	+1.3	-.4
Pension plan	46.0	38.6	2.8	35.2	48.9	+1.8	+3.3	+1.1	+.2	-2.8	-3.2
Savings account	82.4	68.2	8.5	68.8	46.0	90.3	+2.5	0	+.6	+.8	-2.1
Government bonds	39.2	36.4	3.4	33.5	24.4	41.5	43.2	+1.3	+.3	-.1	-2.5
Stocks	22.2	19.3	2.8	22.2	12.5	21.0	11.4	23.3	-.1	+.9	+1.5
Loans lent	10.8	9.1	2.3	10.8	6.3	11.9	5.7	2.8	12.5	+.1	+1.0
Business	6.8	6.8	.6	7.4	1.1	8.0	3.4	2.8	1.1	8.0	-1.7
Debt	41.5	31.8	5.7	32.4	17.6	36.4	15.9	11.4	6.3	1.7	42.6

[a] In percentage points.
[b] Combinations of other bonds (owned by 1.7 percent of the stratum) and annuities (owned by 2.3 percent of the stratum) are omitted because of the small range of d.

that suggested at the beginning of this section, between SUs with large and those with small holdings. As is expected, the former own considerably more variable-dollar assets than the latter.[56]

The similarity of the deviations for comparable combinations in the two tables is somewhat surprising. Although all but one of the deviations are within the range of sampling error, the large deviations occur for the same combinations in both tables, e.g., life insurance-debt, government bonds-debt, pension plans-government bonds, and pension plans-debt. The notable exception is the debt-business relation, the only significant deviation in either table.

The hypotheses outlined earlier about differences in the proportions owning the individual assets are generally supported. But the hypotheses about the nature of the deviations for certain combinations are not. That is, there does not appear to be a strong substitution effect between fixed-dollar assets for SUs with smaller portfolios. Nor does there appear to be strong complementarity for fixed- and variable-dollar assets for this stratum. In general, these tables indicate that operationally the independence hypothesis is as adequate for these subgroups as for the total sample.

As a further test of independence, the "under $25,000" asset stratum was divided into "under $10,000" and "$10,000 to $24,999," and the "$25,000 or more" stratum divided into "$25,000 to $49,999" and "$50,000 or more" in total assets. Analysis of these groups produced results similar to those just outlined. There was no tendency for independence to break down in any one stratum.

Stratification by other characteristics such as income and age produced similar results.

Thus, the general results indicate that the independence hypothesis may be very close to reality for combinations of two assets for the total sample and for subgroups of the sample. The important exceptions are (1) the tendency for complementarity of government bonds and stocks and other assets, and (2) the negative relation between pension plans and businesses.

It must be pointed out that the sample size used in this analysis plays an integral part in the tests of significance and severely limits the amount of stratification which can be done. For example, the tests of significance utilize the standard error of the proportion as a measure of the sampling error. As the stratum size is decreased, the sampling error becomes larger. Under some circumstances, where the maximum possible difference be-

---

[56] It should be emphasized that this difference in ownership rates is not the substitution effect being discussed. The independence (or substitution, or complementarity) effect being tested here is the interaction between assets, not the interaction of assets and SU characteristics.

TABLE 4. PERCENTAGE OF SAMPLE OWNING EACH HOLDING, COMBINATIONS OF TWO HOLDINGS, AND DEVIATIONS[a] BETWEEN ACTUAL AND EXPECTED PERCENTAGES, FOR 146 SAVINGS UNITS WITH $25,000 OR MORE IN TOTAL ASSETS[b]

Holding	Holding										
	Life insurance	Other real estate	Pension plan	Savings account	Government bonds	Other bonds	Stocks	Loans lent	Business	Annuities	Debt
Life insurance..........	87.7	−1.1	+1.8	+1.5	+.9	−.6	+1.0	+2.4	+2.1	+.6	+2.6
Other real estate.......	30.1	35.6	−1.9	+.5	−1.7	+1.4	+.1	0	+1.0	−2.3	+.7
Pension plan..........	43.8	15.1	47.9	+.5	+6.5	+.7	+1.1	−1.0	−5.9	+2.6	−2.0
Savings account........	80.8	32.2	43.8	90.4	+.5	−1.1	−1.0	+.4	−.1	+.3	−.7
Government bonds......	55.5	20.5	36.3	56.8	62.3	+.3	+2.8	−.4	−2.4	+2.5	−3.6
Other bonds...........	14.4	7.5	8.9	14.4	11.0	17.1	+1.9	−.6	+4.1	−.4	+1.9
Stocks	61.6	24.7	34.2	61.6	45.9	13.7	69.2	+1.8	+.5	+1.1	+1.7
Loans lent............	19.2	6.8	8.2	17.8	11.6	2.7	15.1	19.2	−.6	+.1	+.7
Business..............	26.7	11.0	7.5	25.3	15.1	8.9	19.9	4.8	28.1	−.8	+5.6[c]
Annuities.............	9.6	1.4	7.5	9.6	8.9	1.4	8.2	2.1	2.1	10.3	−.1
Debt.................	21.2	8.2	8.2	18.5	9.6	5.5	16.4	4.8	11.6	2.1	21.2

[a] In percentage points.
[b] Combinations of own home (owned by 94.5 percent of the stratum) and checking account (owned by 95.9 percent of the stratum) are omitted because of the small range of d.
[c] Significant at the .05 level.

CHART 1. FREQUENCY DISTRIBUTION OF d^a
FOR ALL COMBINATIONS OF 6 ASSETS

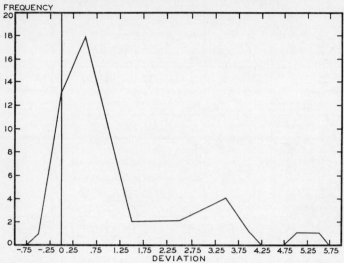

ᵃ In percentage points.

tween A and E is small, it may be mathematically impossible for even
the maximum deviation to be statistically significant. This indicates
the need to look at operational rather than statistical significance when
considering the importance of the deviations. The section on relative
deviation develops this point more fully.

All Combinations

If the independence hypothesis is valid it should hold for combinations of all sizes. Up to this point the discussion has focused on combinations of two assets only. Since it was impracticable to compute all
combinations of 13 assets, 3 fixed-dollar and 3 variable-dollar assets were
selected and all possible combinations of these 6 were investigated. It was
felt that the relationships between savings accounts, government bonds,
loans lent, stocks, businesses, and real estate would be the most sensitive
and would provide the best test of the hypothesis.

The 6 assets, taken 2, 3, 4, 5, and 6 at a time, yield 57 different
combinations. Of the 57 deviations between A and E for these combinations, 5 are negative and 50 are positive. Chart 1 indicates the
same positive bias which is found for all combinations of two assets
shown in Table 2. Although 36 of the 57 deviations are less than 1
percentage point, 7 of the remaining deviations are statistically significant at the .05 level. Chart 2 shows that there is no material difference

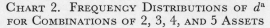

CHART 2. FREQUENCY DISTRIBUTIONS OF d^a
FOR COMBINATIONS OF 2, 3, 4, AND 5 ASSETS

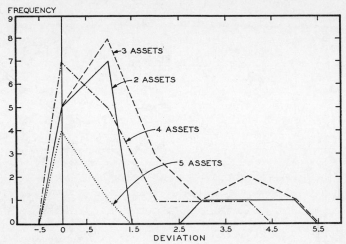

a In percentage points.

in the magnitude of the deviations between combinations of 2, 3, 4, and 5 assets.

Examination of the 7 combinations in which d is significant shows that all contain stocks, 6 contain government bonds and, of course, 6 of the 7 contain both stocks and bonds. This strongly indicates that the greatest positive effect is attributable to one of the two, or both of these assets. In order to tell whether the positive effect is attributable to one of the assets, or to the combination, the number of significant tests can be related to the total number of tests involving each asset or combination. There are 31 combinations involving either government bonds or stocks. About 23 percent of the tests involving stocks are significant and 19 percent of the tests involving government bonds are significant. However, of the 16 tests involving both government bonds and stocks, 44 percent are significant. This indicates that there is a strong complementarity between stocks and government bonds which carries over to combinations containing other assets.

In order to test whether this complementarity holds up when other assets are considered, 9 assets were selected and all possible combinations in which stocks and government bonds appear were investigated. Assets considered in addition to the original 6 are life insurance, pension plans, and own homes.

The 9 assets yield 127 combinations involving stocks, government bonds, and some other asset or assets. Of the 127 deviations computed, 21 are negative, 2 zero, and 104 positive. Thirty-three of the positive

CHART 3. FREQUENCY DISTRIBUTION OF d^a FOR ALL COMBINATIONS
OF 9 ASSETS INCLUDING GOVERNMENT SAVINGS
BONDS AND STOCKS

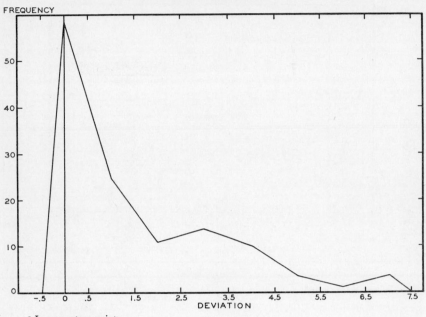

^{a} In percentage points.

deviations are significant at the .05 probability level. Of the 21 negative deviations, none are as large as .5 percent. All of the negative deviations are for some combination involving pension plans, and 19 of the 21 combinations having a negative d include both pension plans and businesses.

It is apparent that the negative relation between pension plans and businesses counteracts the positive relation between stocks and government bonds so that deviations for combinations involving all four assets come very close to zero.

Chart 3 shows a frequency polygon of d for the combinations of 9 assets which is similar to that of all possible combinations of 6 assets shown in Chart 1. However, there are marked differences in the distributions of d when different size combinations are compared. Chart 4 shows that the dispersion of d decreases markedly as the number of assets included in the combination is increased. The modal deviation for 3- and 4-asset combinations is 3.0 percent, while the mode for larger combinations is zero.

These results strongly indicate that for combinations involving stocks, bonds, and other assets, the independence hypothesis is not equally

CHART 4. FREQUENCY DISTRIBUTIONS OF d^a FOR COMBINATIONS OF 3
AND 4, 5 AND 6, AND 7 TO 9 ASSETS INCLUDING GOVERNMENT
SAVINGS BONDS AND STOCKS

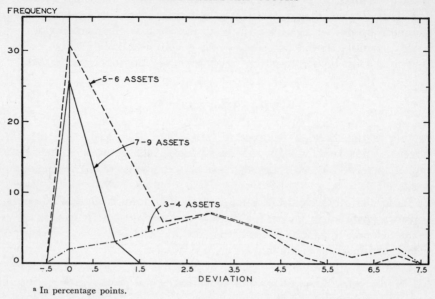

ª In percentage points.

valid for all size combinations. The 33 significant deviations are far
more than could be expected on the basis of chance alone. However,
the independence estimate does provide a close approximation to the
proportion owning a combination in which pensions and businesses are
included and combinations in which there are more than 6 assets.

Relative Deviations

The preceding discussion has been directed entirely at the algebraic
deviation between the actual proportion owning the combination and
the expected value based on independence. From an operational point of
view, however, a measure of the relative deviation may be more meaningful. This is true because the absolute value of d is limited by the
magnitude of the proportions owning each of the assets in the combination. In some cases, where the sample size is relatively small, the
range of d may be smaller than the sampling error. In these cases it is
impossible for even the maximum possible variation to be significant. A
measure of relative deviation can be used as a direct measure of the
forecasting efficiency of the independence estimate as well as another
indication of the reliability of the independence hypothesis. The concept of relative deviation is best explained by example.

If 90 percent — $P(H_1)$ — of the SUs own life insurance and 50 percent — $P(H_2)$ — own government bonds, the maximum deviation of any rational estimate of the proportion owning both from the actual proportion A, is 10 percentage points. The upper limit to A is obviously the minimum proportion owning any one of the assets in the combination — in this example the 50 percent owning government bonds. The lower limit to A must be non-negative and is found by the following formula:

$$(2.4) \qquad L = \sum_{i=1}^{n} P\,(H_i) - (n-1).$$

In this example the lower limit is $L = (.9 + .5) - (2\text{-}1) = .4$ or 40 percent. Consequently, A in this example must be between 40 percent and 50 percent and no rational prediction can be over 10 percentage points off.

If, on the other hand, 50 percent of the SUs own stock and 50 percent own government bonds, the possible range of error is 50 percentage points. Hence, to look at the efficiency of independence as a forecasting technique a measure of the relative error is needed.

Such measure can be computed by relating the algebraic deviation (d) to the total range of possible deviation and converting to percentages to get an index of relative deviation (D). The formula for D is as follows:

$$(2.5) \qquad D = \frac{d}{U-L} \cdot 100 \text{ where}$$

$$d = P\,(H_1, H_2, \ldots, H_n) - P\,(H_1) \cdot P\,(H_2) \cdot \ldots P\,(H_n),$$

$$U = P', \text{ where } P' = \text{the minimum } P\,(H_i), \text{ and}$$

$$L = \sum_{i=1}^{n} P\,(\mathrm{H}_i) - (n-1), \text{ where } L \geq 0.$$

Table 5 gives the relative deviations (D) for all the combinations presented in Table 2. This table shows that for 63 percent of the combinations the actual deviation is less than 10 percent of the total deviation possible. In only 4 of the 78 cases is D as much as 30 percent of the total deviation possible and 3 of the 4 Ds over 30 percent involve stocks in the combination.

Considering all 78 combinations, the mean positive D is $+11.5$ percent and the mean negative D is -6.1 percent. This difference between the mean positive relative deviation and the mean negative relative deviation supports the conclusions arrived at on the basis of tests of significance and the signs of the deviations, i.e., there is a slight bias toward complementarity between assets. This complementarity leads to

TABLE 5. RELATIVE DEVIATIONS[a] FOR ALL COMBINATIONS OF TWO HOLDINGS, FOR 384 SAVINGS UNITS

Holding	Holding												
	Life insurance	Own home	Other real estate	Checking account	Pension plan	Savings account	Government bonds	Other bonds	Stocks	Loans lent	Business	Annuities	Debt
Life insurance........		+14	+ 4	− 4	− 8	+ 7	− 1	− 5	− 1	+ 2	+ 9	+ 3	+19
Own home...........			+10	+14	+20	+12	+30	− 5	+11	− 9	+12	− 3	− 6
Other real estate.....				+20	− 9	− 2	+ 4	+10	+14	+ 5	+ 5	−11	− 3
Checking account.....					− 8	+ 1	+20	+ 1	+38[b]	+ 1	+14	+ 9	− 9
Pension plan.........						+11	+10	− 1	+ 1	+ 1	−26[b]	+24	− 6
Savings account......							+12	− 2	− 1	+ 5	− 1	+ 3	− 8
Government bonds.....								+ 9	+11[b]	+ 4	+ 2	+29	−13[b]
Other bonds.........									+33[b]	0	+24[b]	+ 9	− 6
Stocks..............										+10	+15[b]	+31[b]	− 4
Loans lent...........											+ 1	+ 4	− 2
Business............												− 6	− 4
Annuities...........													0
Debt...............													

[a] In percentages.

[b] Statistically significant at the .05 level.

approximately twice as many positive deviations as negative ones, and the mean positive D is approximately twice the size of the mean negative D. A very slight tendency toward a positive bias holds even if stocks, government bonds, and checking accounts are not considered. The mean positive and negative Ds for all combinations (except those involving stocks, government bonds, checking accounts, and debt) are $+8.6$ percent and -6.2 percent respectively.

It is apparent that the independence hypothesis is not equally efficient in predicting combinations of all assets. Relatively speaking, the greatest errors are for government bonds, stocks, and checking accounts. Mean Ds, disregarding signs, for these assets are 12 percent, 13 percent, and 12 percent respectively. The smallest relative errors are for loans lent, savings accounts, and life insurance — the mean Ds are 3 percent, 6 percent, and 6 percent respectively.

In general these results indicate that, in the aggregate at least, the independence hypothesis is a relatively efficient means of predicting proportions owning most combinations of two assets. However, a slight tendency toward complementarity persists for all combinations of assets and the mean relative deviation varies somewhat for different assets.

Relative deviations corresponding to the combinations presented in Tables 3 and 4 were also computed. In general, the same results were obtained. There were no marked differences in the means for any stratum. For example, the average errors, disregarding signs, for those with less than $25,000 in total assets and those with $25,000 or more are 9.5 percent and 8.9 percent respectively (the comparable mean for the total sample is 9.4 percent). In addition, relative deviations were computed for subgroups of the sample after it had been stratified by income. Again, parallel results were obtained.

Corrections for Independence Estimates

The foregoing results strongly indicate that the independence hypothesis provides a reasonably efficient forecasting technique of proportions owning various combinations of assets. The major exceptions are combinations involving government bonds and stocks. In this case, independence estimates run consistently below the actual proportions. This consistent underestimation suggests that it may be possible to use some correction procedure to adjust the independence estimate and thereby obtain an unbiased and consistent estimate of the actual proportion owning the combination.

As an illustration of one way to correct the independence estimate, the expected value and the actual value of all combinations of government bonds, stocks, and seven other assets, which were discussed on page

38, have been treated as a regression problem in the following analysis. If independence prevails, a scatter diagram with A plotted on the ordinate and E on the abscissa would show points randomly distributed about a 45-degree line running from the lower left-hand corner to the upper right-hand corner of the graph. The regression equation for such a line would be: (2.6) $A = a + bE + u$, where $a = 0$ and $b = 1$. The actual scatter diagram for the 127 combinations involving stocks and government bonds shows a clear pattern running from the origin at a slope greater than one. The equation for the regression line fitted to this distribution of points by the least-squares method is

$$(2.7) \qquad\qquad A' = .53 + 1.31(E).$$

The regression coefficient is significantly different from unity ($T = 16.4$). The coefficient of determination is .97. Using this regression equation, a corrected estimate of A can be obtained by inserting any given value of E into the equation.

For example, if 50 percent of the sample own government bonds and 50 percent own stock, the unadjusted independence estimate of the proportion (A) owning both would be 25 percent. However, the adjusted point estimate (A') is 33.3 percent. This proportion is found in the following way:

$$(2.8) \qquad\qquad A' = .53 + 1.31 \,(25)$$
$$A' = 33.3.$$

Independence of Dollar Amounts

The preceding discussion has centered on the independence of asset ownership. No mention has been made of the amounts held in the various assets. If the ownership of two assets is independent but the amounts held in the assets are closely correlated, the independence hypothesis loses much of its operational significance. Hence, the preceding analysis needs to be supported by an analysis of the dollar amounts held in various combinations of assets.

In order to determine the degree of the relation between typical combinations of assets, two fixed-dollar assets (savings accounts and government bonds) and two variable-dollar assets (stocks and real estate) were selected and regression analyses made of the amounts held in combinations of these four.

Scatter diagrams of the variables made on both arithmetic and logarithmic grids failed to show persistent patterns for any of the combinations. However, regression equations were fitted to the data to determine the degree of relationship actually present. A log-log transformation was used to minimize the effect of some of the extreme values

TABLE 6. RESULTS OF THE REGRESSION ANALYSES OF AMOUNTS HELD
IN SELECTED ASSETS

Y	X	r^2_{yx}	b_{yx}	σb	N
Government bonds	Savings accounts	.122	+.348[a]	.072	169
Stock	Savings accounts	.048	+.252[a]	.098	134
Stock	Government bonds	.019	+.168	.133	86
Real estate	Stock	.127	+.306[a]	.126	43

[a] Significant at the .05 level.

on the over-all regression (market value of stock varied from under $100 to over $1,000,000). The results of the regressions are presented in Table 6.

Table 6 clearly shows that the degree of correlation (r^2_{yx}) between the dollar amounts held in the various assets is negligible. In no case was as much as 14 percent of the total variation explained by the use of the regression equation. The regression coefficients (b_{yx}) indicate that the relations may be slightly positive, but with less than 14 percent of the variation accounted for, it is extremely hazardous to place any reliance on these statistics.

The relation between government bonds and stocks is somewhat surprising. This is the one regression which was not significantly different from zero although it was based on 86 observations and tests of independence of ownership indicated a positive relation. Apparently the positive relationship between ownership of the two assets does not carry over to amounts held in the two.

Summary

In conclusion, the analysis of the ownership of combinations of two assets, combinations of n assets, measures of relative deviation, and correlation of dollar amounts held in various combinations of assets, when applied to the total sample and to subgroups, all form a pervasive pattern indicating a slight tendency toward complementarity between assets. However, this tendency is not pronounced and from an operational point of view the independence hypothesis appears to be a close approximation to reality.

III. AN EXPLANATION OF INDEPENDENCE

In the preceding chapter evidence was presented which, with certain qualifications, supported a hypothesis of independence in the ownership of selected assets making up consumer savings portfolios. The present chapter is an attempt to offer an explanation of why the independence hypothesis may be valid.

The first impression one gets from the independence hypothesis is that it must contradict the orthodox theory of consumer choice, i.e., it implies that consumers do not consider the substitutability of various assets in determining the composition of their portfolios and that the ownership of one asset (or combination of assets) does not affect the likelihood of owning other assets. This in turn implies that consumers irrationally fail to consider assets they currently own when deciding where to place additional funds they have saved. However, this explanation is not the only, or the most meaningful, way to account for the independence phenomenon. A second and more reasonable explanation is possible without postulating irrational behavior on the part of the consumer.

A Restatement of the Independence Hypothesis

First, additional refinement of the concept of independence is needed. Assets are not just held "in general." People have motives for holding assets and perceptions of the suitability of specific assets for each of the motives. However, the model of portfolio selection becomes complicated because the acquisition of one asset may satisfy any one of a number of motives, and one motive may be satisfied by any of a number of assets. Thus, it is entirely possible for two assets to be substitutes on one dimension (for one motive) and complementary, or independent, on other dimensions. Consequently, in referring to substitutability or complementarity it is essential to specify whether one is referring to a single dimension (motive) or to all dimensions.

Using elementary probability theory it is possible to derive necessary and sufficient conditions for independence of assets in terms of the motives for holding assets, and then test whether the empirical data satisfy these conditions. The approach is to state the proportions holding each asset and each combination of assets in terms of the proportions holding the asset(s) for any or all of the motives.[57]

Assume for the sake of brevity and ease of notation that there are two assets (a) and (b), and each can be held for either or both of two motives (i) and (j).[58]

The independence hypothesis developed in Chapter II is

(3.1) $P(ab) = P(a) P(b)$ where

$P(a)$ = the proportion of the sample owning asset a,

$P(b)$ = the proportion of the sample owning asset b, and

$P(ab)$ = the proportion of the sample owning asset a and asset b.

However, if the distribution of motives for holding the assets are taken into consideration, the proportions must be stated differently. Thus,

(3.2) $P(a) = P(a_i) + P(a_j) - P(a_{ij})$,

(3.3) $P(b) = P(b_i) + P(b_j) - P(b_{ij})$, and

(3.4) $P(ab) = P(a_i b_i) + P(a_i b_j) + P(a_j b_i) + P(a_j b_j)$
$$+ P(a_{ij} b_{ij}) - P(a_i b_{ij}) - P(a_j b_{ij}) - P(a_{ij} b_i)$$
$$- P(a_{ij} b_j).$$

Equation (3.2) is interpreted as follows: the proportion owning asset a is the sum of the proportions owning asset a for motive i and for motive j, minus the proportion owning a for both i and j. $P(a_{ij})$ is counted twice, once in $P(a_i)$ and once in $P(a_j)$; hence, it must be subtracted once from the total. Equation (3.3) is a similar statement for asset b. Equation (3.4) is the corollary of (3.2) and (3.3) for the proportion owning both a and b.

For the independence hypothesis to be true, the product of the right-hand side of equations (3.2) and (3.3) must be equal to the right-hand side of equation (3.4). Thus,

(3.5) $[P(a_i) + P(a_j) - P(a_{ij})] [P(b_i) + P(b_j) - P(b_{ij})]$
$$= P(a_i b_i) + P(a_i b_j) + P(a_j b_i) + P(a_j b_j) + P(a_{ij} b_{ij})$$
$$- P(a_i b_{ij}) - P(a_j b_{ij}) - P(a_{ij} b_i) - P(a_{ij} b_j).$$

---

[57] For the probability theory behind this approach and the proof of its generality, see William Feller, *An Introduction to Probability Theory and Its Applications* (2nd ed.; New York: Wiley, 1957), Vol. 1, pp. 88-91.

[58] It should be pointed out that this discussion is carried out in terms of two assets and two motives but the solution is general since asset (a) may be regarded as one asset and asset (b) as any combination of other assets; and similarly, motive (i) as one motive and motive (j) as any or all other motives.

If the following conditions are satisfied, it can be proven that equation (3.5) *must* be true, i.e., that $P(ab) = P(a) P(b)$ (see Appendix B).

Condition 1:

(3.6) $P(a_i b_i) = P(a_i) P(b_i),$

(3.6a) $P(a_i b_j) = P(a_i) P(b_j),$

(3.6b) $P(a_j b_i) = P(a_j) P(b_i),$ and

(3.6c) $P(a_j b_j) = P(a_j) P(b_j).$

Condition 2:

(3.7) $P(a_{ij} b_i) = P(a_{ij}) P(b_i),$

(3.7a) $P(a_{ij} b_j) = P(a_{ij}) P(b_j),$

(3.7b) $P(a_i b_{ij}) = P(a_i) P(b_{ij}),$ and

(3.7c) $P(a_j b_{ij}) = P(a_j) P(b_{ij}).$

However, Conditions 1 and 2 are merely sufficient conditions and are not necessary for independence. A necessary and sufficient condition is for the sum of the terms on the left side of equation (3.5) to be equal to the sum of the terms on the right side of equation (3.5). Thus, independence may still prevail if the motives are distributed in such a way that all the parts of Conditions 1 and 2 are not satisfied, but the following is:

Condition 3:

(3.8) $[P(a_i) + P(a_j) - P(a_{ij})] [P(b_i) + P(b_j) - P(b_{ij})]$
         $= P(a_i b_i) + P(a_i b_j) + P(a_j b_i) + P(a_j b_j) + P(a_{ij} b_{ij})$
         $- P(a_i b_{ij}) - P(a_j b_{ij}) - P(a_{ij} b_i) - P(a_{ij} b_j).$

Further Empirical Tests

Only limited data are available at this time to test the empirical validity of Conditions 1, 2, and 3. In one segment of the sample respondents were asked to give their reasons for holding selected assets. The respondents were asked to give any of 7 listed motives (or other motives) for holding each of 9 assets. The results obtained from 175 SUs can be used as a first indication of the validity of Conditions 1, 2, and 3.

Testing all possible combinations of 9 assets held for all combinations of 8 reasons would mean a prohibitive number of tests; consequently, certain restrictions had to be made. First, only the four most frequently held assets and the most frequently given reasons for holding each were considered. This restriction reduced the number of items to 15; however, the possible combinations still numbered in the thousands. Consequently, the number of tests was further restricted to the two following cases: all combinations of two assets, each held for one motive or all motives; and all combinations of three assets, each held for one motive. The first case resulted in 81 combinations and the second in 102 combinations.

Table 7 gives the deviations of the expected value from the actual value for the 81 tests made of combinations of two motives. Of the 81 deviations, 43 are negative, 37 are positive, and 1 equals zero. Over 43 percent of the deviations are less than 1 percentage point and only 4 deviations are larger than ± 3.2 percentage points. Only 3 deviations are statistically significant at the 95 percent probability level. Out of this number of tests one would expect approximately 4 tests to be significant owing to chance alone.

Of the 102 tests made of combinations of three reasons, there were 43 positive, 50 negative, and 9 zero deviations. About 94 percent of the deviations were within ± 1.2 percentage points and all were within ± 2 percentage points. None of the deviations was statistically significant. It should be pointed out that the maximum value of d in 40 of the tests is 6.3 percent. For these cases statistical significance loses much of its relevancy. However, in none of the tests was d as much as 23 percent of the total possible variation between the actual proportion and the expected proportion. Consequently, it is apparent that the independence estimate is close to the actual proportion.

Chart 5 shows a frequency polygon of d for the 81 combinations of two, the 102 combinations of three, and the total 183 combinations. It is clear from this graph that there is a difference in dispersion depending on the size of the combinations. However, all of the lines in the chart center about the zero value.

These results support Conditions 1 and 2 listed on page 48. However, the pattern of the signs indicates that independence may actually hold, not because each of the parts of Conditions 1 and 2 is satisfied, but because negative deviations on one dimension are cancelled by positive deviations on another. For example, Table 7 shows that the ownership of savings accounts for income is complementary to the ownership of stock for all reasons and for each of the reasons taken separately. In contrast, the ownership of savings accounts for old age security is negatively related to stock held for all reasons and for each of the reasons taken separately.

In either event (whether Conditions 1 and 2 hold, or only Condi-

TABLE 7. PERCENTAGE OF SAMPLE OWNING ASSETS FOR SELECTED MOTIVES AND DEVIATIONS[a] BETWEEN ACTUAL AND EXPECTED PERCENTAGES FOR 81 COMBINATIONS OF TWO ASSETS, FOR 175 SAVINGS UNITS

Holding and motive	Savings accounts				Life insurance				Government bonds			Stocks			
	Yield	Safety	Li-quidity	Old age	All mo-tives	Safety	Old age	Educa-tion	All mo-tives	Old age	Patri-otism	All mo-tives	Yield	Hedge	Old age
Savings accounts[b]															
Yield	36.0				−1.3	− .3	−2.9	−1.8	+ .3	− .5	+1.7	+1.1	+ .1	+2.7	+2.6
Safety		39.0			+1.1	−1.0	− .6	+ .1	−3.2	− .6	− .2	−5.2[c]	+2.2	− .6	+ .3
Liquidity			22.3		−1.4	− .9	−1.8	+ .5	+ .5	−1.7	−1.4	−2.8	+1.9	+2.3	+1.1
Old age				31.4	+1.4	−2.0	−1.5	−1.0	− .4	+2.6	+ .3	−5.7[c]	− .4	− .9	− .8
Life insurance															
All motives					90.9				− .9	−1.0	+ .6	−2.5	0	+ .3	− .4
Safety						24.6			+ .5	− .9	+ .2	+1.0	− .1	−1.4	− .9
Old age							59.1		+ .8	+5.9[c]	+2.7	+1.3	+4.0	−2.5	−1.2
Education								16.0		−2.4	−1.0		− .8	+ .7	−1.0
Government bonds															
All motives									59.4			− .5	+ .3	+1.9	+2.6
Old age										20.6		+2.6	.2	−2.1	+1.3
Patriotism											6.3		.9	+ .5	+1.1
Stocks															
All motives												38.3			
Yield													12.0		
Hedge														10.3	
Old age															8.0

[a] In percentage points.
[b] All motives omitted because all SUs owned savings accounts.
[c] Statistically significant at the .05 level.

CHART 5. FREQUENCY DISTRIBUTIONS OF DEVIATIONS[a] BETWEEN ACTUAL
AND EXPECTED PERCENTAGES FOR COMBINATIONS OF TWO ASSETS,
EACH HELD FOR ONE OR ALL MOTIVES; AND COMBINATIONS
OF THREE ASSETS, EACH HELD FOR ONE MOTIVE

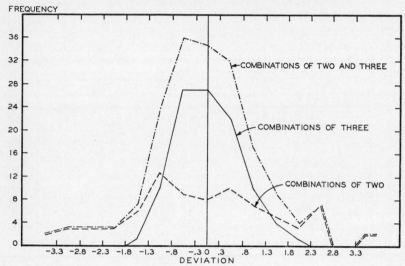

FREQUENCY

[a] In percentage points.

tion 3 holds) the results clearly show that emphasis must be placed on
the distribution and interaction of motives and on individual perceptions
of assets.

These results point up the need for a conceptual framework or theory
of behavior which will provide an understanding of the way motives are
distributed and the way they may be related to the assets. Psychological
field theory, as developed by Kurt Lewin, provides just such a framework.[59]

Field Theory

The basic premise of field theory is that all behavior is determined

[59] Only the bare essentials of field theory necessary for understanding the portfolio problem are presented here. It is beyond the scope of this study to make a
complete review of the theory and its ramifications. Lewin's major works are
Principles of Topological Psychology (1st ed.; New York: McGraw-Hill, 1936);
The Conceptual Representation and the Measurement of Psychological Forces
(Durham: Duke University Press, 1938); "Behavior and Development as a Function of the Total Situation" in Leonard Carmichael, ed., *Manual of Child Psychology* (New York: Wiley, 1946); and *Field Theory in Social Science,* edited by
Dorwin Cartwright (1st ed.; New York: Harper, 1951).
    A detailed review of the work of Lewin and its application to marketing and
consumer behavior is found in Reavis Cox and Wroe Alderson, *Theory in Marketing* (Homewood: Irwin, 1950), pp. 41-63.

by the total situation.[60] That is, any given action is determined by all of the factors, both from within the individual and from the environment, acting on the individual at that instant. Stated another way, behavior (B) is a function of the life-space (Lsp) of the individual, where life-space of the individual is made up of two interacting systems — the individual (I) and the environment (E). However, there are intervening steps and hypothetical constructs which are essential to the understanding of the behavior of the individual. The individual's present condition and his perception of environment give rise to certain psychic tensions. The tensions may be likened to motives, needs, or desires. The tensions may be brought about by physiological changes within the individual (e.g., hunger) or by decisions (e.g., the desire for recreation).

At any given moment in time the individual has a structure of these tensions pressing for release. At that same moment the individual perceives goal regions (objects, other individuals, or even social groups) which have either positive or negative valences (or both). Not all goal regions have the same valence, i.e., they are not equally attractive or unattractive. Conflicts arise because the same goal regions have both positive and negative valences or because two goal regions have equal positive valences. However, it is the counterbalancing of all of the forces, i.e., the total tension structure and the total valences, which produces locomotion (behavior) toward one or a combination of the goals. The attainment of the goal reduces the tension and a new system is created. Thus, the individual is in a constant teleostatic process and the goal sought is a broad biosocial equilibrium.

In field theory the importance of perception and rational problem-solving behavior is emphasized; but it is important to note that there may be discrepancies between the perceived environment and the real environment. However, the perceived environment is the important variable since to the individual it *is* the real environment and he reacts according to it.

If one views the problem of portfolio selection in this frame of reference it is no longer surprising that the aggregate joint distribution of motives for holding assets and perceptions of assets is found to be approximately independent. And, as the proof on page 48 has shown, if this distribution is independent, the aggregate distribution of assets held for all reasons will be independent.

A Model of Portfolio Selection

A general model of portfolio selection can be developed within this

---

[60] The following discussion is based largely on K. B. Madsen, *Theories of Motivation* (Copenhagen: Munksgaard, 1959), pp. 120-34.

framework. For example, at any given time an individual who has a given stock of savings is faced with alternative ways of holding the funds. The way in which he holds the funds depends on the array of motives and the valences of the goal regions. The motives may be any one of the multitude of conditions he desires, e.g., increased income now or in the future, a hedge against inflation, a liquid fund for emergencies, the status or prestige of belonging to an investment club, a fund that is guaranteed safe in principal, a fund for old age, shelter provided by his own home, and so on. These motives are a function of his life-space, i.e., of the total situation within himself and his perceived environment such as age, health, family responsibility, total dollars saved, income, education, past conditioning, attitudes, expectations, aspirations, perceptions of financial and economic conditions, and interest rates.

The complexity of the distribution of motives is not the only factor responsible for the ultimate distribution of assets owned. Another important factor is the discrepancy between the real and the perceived environment. Not all individuals have perfect knowledge of the true nature of the assets and there are individual differences in the perception of the nature of specific assets. These differences in perception are important in determining the aggregate asset ownership distribution. For example, assume it were possible to find two individuals, I_1 and I_2, with the same motive structure, M_{12}. Let the motive structure consist of a desire for increased income and guaranteed safety of the principal of the savings fund. Assume also, that both I_1 and I_2 perceive government bonds as the safest asset and stocks as the optimal vehicle for income. However, I_1's perception of stocks differs markedly from that of I_2. I_1 believes that stocks can only go up in the long run. There may be day-to-day variations in the market price of the stock, but the long-run growth of the economy and the government's commitment to full employment mean that equities will not depreciate in value. Even though he is certain stocks will not go down, funds invested in stocks are not actually guaranteed; consequently he may place some of his funds in government bonds and some in stocks to satisfy both motives.

Now, assume that I_2's perception of stocks is that they are good income-producing assets but that they are as likely to go down in value as up. Hence, placing funds in stocks is incompatible with his motive for guaranteed safety. As a consequence, I_2 may forgo the optimal income vehicle and acquire a federally insured savings and loan account because it has a higher yield than government savings bonds and is still compatible with his desire for safety.

Thus, two different portfolios have resulted from the same motives, because of differences in perceptions of the applicability of specific assets to certain motives. Now, assume I_1 and I_2 acquire a third motive — patriotism or a sense of obligation to buy government bonds. I_1 has already acquired the bonds; hence, no change in his portfolio is required. However, I_2 is motivated to acquire the bonds and his portfolio now consists of savings and loan accounts and government bonds. I_2 may consider the assets he holds as close substitutes on many dimensions, but he acquired both because he perceived differences in the capacity of the assets to satisfy some of the motives.

It is not surprising that the multitude of forces acting on individuals create a structure of motives and perceptions which, when aggregated over all individuals or even over homogeneous socioeconomic groups, approaches independence.

The simple model which has just been developed can be stated symbolically as follows: let,

(3.9) $\qquad M_i = f_1 \, (Lsp)_i =$ the motive structure of the ith individual, and

(3.10) $\qquad H_i = f_2 \, (M)_i =$ the assets held by the ith individual (i.e., portfolio composition).

The tests of significance described on pages 48 and 49 indicate that the aggregate distribution — $\sum_{i=1}^{h} [f_2(M)_i]$ — on the left side of the equation (3.10) is approximately independent.

Also Conditions 1, 2, and 3 show that if this distribution is independent, the aggregate distribution of assets — $\sum_{i=1}^{h} H_i$ — must also be independent.

Conclusions

The following conclusions can be drawn from the investigation of the asset composition of consumer savings portfolios.

(1) The aggregate distribution of assets for the total sample and for subgroups of the sample approximates that which would be found if the ownership of assets were independent. The independence estimate appears to be operationally significant since the great majority of the estimates are extremely close to the actual proportions. Although there is a slight tendency toward complementarity of assets, particularly for combinations involving government bonds and stocks, the over-all result closely approximates that which would be found if there were no interactions among assets.

(2) There is no need to postulate irrationality on the part of the consumers to explain the independence result. Rather the explanation is found in the complex structures of individuals' motives, the multidimen-

sional nature of assets, and the fact that not all people perceive their environment alike.

(3) Independence or the approximation of it means that in determining the demand for a given asset, or for a combination of assets, unbiased and consistent estimates of the parameters should be obtainable without specifying interaction effects between assets or between motives.

(4) If the proportions owning individual assets are known, proportions owning, or not owning, various combinations of assets can be predicted using the independence hypothesis and corrections if they are needed.

Limitations

There are several limitations to the conclusions arrived at here. First, it must be emphasized that the sample used is a very select one. There is a definite high income, high asset ownership bias. It is composed of SUs in two large metropolitan areas. Hence, it cannot be considered as representative of the general population.

The study is a cross-section analysis of one point in time, early spring of 1960, and may not be applicable to other points in time.

Problems of response error may also affect the conclusions arrived at here. However, these influences are probably the minimum possible in any existing body of data on consumer savings, since validation data were available and were utilized to correct known biases before the analysis was made. Nonetheless, it is possible that patterns of nonreporting could influence the results.

The statistical tests of significance are not exact. Finally, the sample available severely restricts the conclusions which can be drawn in many cases. It is quite likely that if the sample had been three or four times as large, the study of subdivisions of the sample and of less frequently held combinations of assets also might have produced interesting results.

PART THREE

THE FIXED-DOLLAR VERSUS VARIABLE-DOLLAR
COMPOSITION OF PORTFOLIOS

IV. DEVELOPMENT OF THE MODEL

The importance of the fixed- versus variable-dollar composition of consumer savings portfolios and some of its effects on individuals, financial institutions, and general economic and financial conditions were pointed out in the introductory chapter. The purpose of this part of the study is to provide information about this aspect of portfolio composition. The basic objective here is to find out what factors are associated with variations in the variable-dollar composition of consumer savings portfolios and what is the nature of their influence.

The analysis is carried out using two different measures of variable-dollar composition. The first measure, V, is the percentage of SUs' total savings which is held in variable-dollar assets, excluding only currency and the cash value of pension plans and life insurance.[61] The second measure, V^*, is similar to the first except for the exclusion of the balances of checking accounts and equity in owner-occupied homes from total assets and the exclusion of equity in owner-occupied homes from total variable-dollar assets.

The first measure gives a reasonably close approximation of the composition of total portfolios but is somewhat biased toward variable-dollar assets since the excluded assets are all fixed-dollar in nature. The second measure gives an approximation of the composition of the discretionary portfolio, i.e., that part of the portfolio which is independent of the SU's demand for transaction balances and housing, and in which the SU can

---

[61] The cash value of pension plans and life insurance and the amount of currency on hand were omitted because of the extreme difficulty in obtaining these figures from the majority of the SUs. Although most of the SUs know the face value of their life insurance policies and the probable monthly retirement benefits from their pension plans, very few know the present cash value of either asset. In the computation of V and V^*, debts which could be related to specific assets were deducted from those assets before obtaining the total amount of fixed- and variable-dollar assets, e.g., the outstanding amounts of mortgages and home improvement loans were deducted from the value of real estate, and so forth. Since the asset value of consumer durables was excluded from the analysis, the debt on these assets was not deducted from total savings. In addition, no adjustments were made for 20 debts which could not be related to any specific asset. A separate investigation made of the adjusted dependent variables indicates that the net effect of the omission is negligible.

exercise considerable discretion in management. Analysis on this level may yield additional information about the more sensitive components of consumers' portfolios.

The General Model

In the preceding chapter a general, though simple, model was presented which made portfolio composition a function of the condition of the individual and his perception of the environment. In the development of this model the multidimensional nature of assets, the complex structure of motives for holding assets, and the differences in individual perceptions of assets were stressed. Formulating the problem of this chapter in the framework of that model contributes to the understanding of the nature of the problem and the techniques necessary to analyze it.

For example, let

$(Lsp)_i$ = the life-space of the ith individual, where i = 1, 2, 3, . . . , h,

M_i = the motive structure of the ith individual,

$\sum_{k=1}^{n} H_{ki}$ = the total savings of the ith individual in dollars held in all n assets,

$\sum_{v=1}^{r} H_{vi}$ = total dollars held in r variable-dollar assets by the ith individual, and

$\sum_{f=1}^{s} H_{fi}$ = total dollars held in fixed-dollar assets by the ith individual.

Then, (4.1) follows by definition.

$$(4.1) \qquad \sum_{k=1}^{n} H_{ki} = \sum_{v=1}^{r} H_{vi} + \sum_{f=1}^{s} H_{fi}.$$

The proportion of total savings held in variable-dollar assets can now be stated as a function of the motive structure. And since the motive structure is a function of the life-space of the individual, the behavior variable — selection of a certain variable-dollar composition — can be stated as another function of the life-space of the individual.

Thus,

$$(4.2) \qquad \frac{\sum_{v=1}^{r} H_{vi}}{\sum_{k=1}^{n} H_{ki}} = f_1 (M_i) = f_2 (Lsp_i).$$

The analysis carried out in the preceding chapters also indicated that the interaction between assets and the interaction between motives can be disregarded; hence, the major problem is to isolate and correctly specify the factors in the life-space of the individual which are relevant to the variable-dollar composition of the portfolio. The foregoing analysis was also based on the premise that all of the factors, acting together, determine behavior. Thus, some form of multivariate analysis is clearly needed.

The approach taken here is to make the percentage of total savings held in variable-dollar assets the dependent variable in a multivariate regression analysis. This technique makes possible several different measures of the association between the dependent and independent variables. For example, the coefficient of multiple determination (R^2) gives a percentage measure of the degree of association. The coefficients of net regression give a measure of the nature of the relation between each of the independent variables and the dependent variable, and the standardized regression coefficients provide a measure of the relative importance of each of the independent variables. In the general case the regression function used throughout the following analysis is

$$(4.3) \qquad X_1 = a_o + a_2 X_2 + a_3 X_3 + \ldots + a_n X_n + u$$

where,

$$X_1 = \frac{\sum H_v}{\sum H_k} (100) = \text{the percentage of savings held in variable-dollar assets; and}$$

$$X_2, X_3, \ldots, X_n = \text{relevant SU characteristics.}$$

Selection of the Independent Variables

The most difficult problem in the analysis is the selection of the proper independent variables $(X_2, \ldots, X_n)$ to be included in the function and to correctly specify their relation to the dependent variables. The selection of the correct variables must be based on a priori reasoning, theory, and available data since it is neither practical nor possible to include in the model all of the factors which may influence the SU's determination of portfolio composition.

Review of Asset Characteristics

A careful analysis of the characteristics of the assets classified in the fixed- and variable-dollar categories is needed before the relevant SU characteristics can be specified. The fixed-dollar category includes the following assets: checking accounts, savings and loan shares, savings accounts and certificates in commercial banks and mutual savings banks, postal savings, credit union shares, government savings bonds, the cash value of annuities, and the outstanding balances of loans and mortgages lent.

The variable-dollar category includes common and preferred stocks, shares in mutual funds, shares in investment clubs, brokerage accounts, corporate and other bonds, marketable government securities, equity in business, equity in owner-occupied homes, and equity in other real estate.

Assets in the fixed-dollar category are, in general, more liquid,[62] safer,[63] more convenient to acquire, have greater divisibility, and have more stable yields than assets in the variable-dollar category.[64] Thus, assets in the fixed-dollar category are of a more conservative nature and subject the holder to less risk of illiquidity, loss of principal, and fluctuation in yield. However, fixed-dollar assets make the holder more susceptible to the purchasing power risk, i.e., loss in the real value of the asset due to increase in the general price level.

On the other hand, variable-dollar assets may provide the holder with some protection against the purchasing power risk. This is true because variable-dollar assets have an opportunity to appreciate in value along with increases in the general price level. Variable-dollar assets also provide the holder with an opportunity for greater yield, but the certainty of the yield is likely to be less in most instances. In general, variable-dollar assets require of the holder a greater degree of financial sophistication, more time and trouble in management, and a larger initial commitment of funds; and in some cases they represent a way of life (e.g., home ownership versus renting).

Selection of SU Characteristics

The comparison of the two types of holdings suggests several hypotheses about the factors which may influence SUs' decisions about portfolio composition. These hypotheses can be conveniently grouped in two broad categories — those dealing with the financial condition of the SU and those dealing with nonfinancial or socio-psychological and demographic characteristics of the SU.

Financial Condition

The financial condition of the SU may be thought of as having two dimensions — one of financial ability or capacity and one of financial needs or demands. A priori reasoning, based on the fundamental nature of the two kinds of assets being studied here, leads one to expect a positive relationship between financial ability and the proportion of total savings held in variable-dollar form and a negative relationship between financial

---

[62] Especially if liquidity is construed as ease of convertibility to a relatively *fixed* number of dollars.

[63] For example, most commercial banks and savings and loan institutions have deposits protected by federal insurance, and government savings bonds are guaranteed by the federal government itself.

[64] Of course, there may be exceptions to the general case, e.g., some loans lent may be less liquid than some stocks and marketable government securities.

TABLE 8. PERCENTAGE OF TOTAL SAVINGS HELD IN VARIABLE-DOLLAR ASSETS, BY TOTAL SAVINGS, FOR 330 SAVINGS UNITS

Total savings	Percentage						Base
	0–19	20–39	40–59	60–79	80–100	Total	
Under $1,000...............	86	7	7			100	14
$1,000–$4,999..............	42	10		29	19	100	31
$5,000–$9,999..............	12	2	5	29	52	100	42
$10,000–$24,999............	5	5	14	34	42	100	94
$25,000–$49,999............	1	12	18	28	41	100	74
$50,000–$99,999............		5	12	19	63	99[a]	41
$100,000 and over..........			9	9	82	100	34
	11	6	11	26	46	100	330

[a] Does not add to 100 percent because of rounding.

needs and the same dependent variable. However, obtaining the appropriate measures or indexes of financial ability and needs is difficult. Accumulated savings, one variable representing financial ability, is of obvious importance in portfolio decisions, for without some accumulation of funds it is impossible for the SU to exercise effective demand for any type of holding. As this form of financial ability increases one would expect a greater amount of emphasis to be placed on variable-dollar assets. For example, virtually all SUs need a safe, liquid fund which can be used in the event of an emergency. If the SU has only a small amount of savings, the need for an emergency fund could be expected to take priority over other needs. However, as the SU increases its savings the relative importance of the emergency fund is likely to diminish and variable-dollar assets are more likely to be added to the portfolio.

Differences in the divisibility of fixed- and variable-dollar assets also leads one to expect a direct relationship between total assets and the proportion of savings held in variable-dollar assets. Holdings such as checking accounts, savings accounts, and government bonds can be acquired by very small commitments of funds, i.e., they are nearly perfectly divisible, whereas corporate and other bonds usually come in denominations of $1,000; odd-lot purchases of stocks involve a higher commission than round lots; and the purchase of a home or other real estate requires a large commitment of funds.[65]

A cross-classification table of V and total assets clearly supports this hypothesis. Table 8 shows that the proportion of total assets held in

[65] Of course, low down payments on homes and other real estate make it possible to acquire these assets with only a fraction of the purchase price in cash. Even so, the down payment is substantially larger than the amount needed to acquire any of the fixed-dollar assets.

variable-dollar form increases directly with the size of the total savings. Over 80 percent of the SUs with less than $1,000 in total assets have less than 20 percent of their savings in variable-dollar form, while approximately the same proportion (82 percent) of those with over $100,000 in total assets have more than 80 percent of their savings in variable-dollar form. The table also shows that the percentage of the SUs who hold predominantly fixed-dollar assets decreases steadily, and the percentage of SUs who hold predominantly variable-dollar assets increases steadily, as the asset level increases. These results are similar to those found in other studies (see page 14).

The cross-classification table of V^* and total discretionary assets (total assets less equity in owner-occupied homes and balances in checking accounts) shows a similar pattern to that presented in Table 8. However, the distribution of V^* is considerably different from that of V. Table 8 shows that 72 percent of the SUs hold at least 60 percent of their total funds in variable-dollar assets; Table 9 shows that only 38 percent of the

TABLE 9. PERCENTAGE OF TOTAL DISCRETIONARY SAVINGS HELD
IN VARIABLE-DOLLAR ASSETS, BY TOTAL DISCRETIONARY
SAVINGS, FOR 330 SAVINGS UNITS

Total discretion- ary savings	Percentage						Base
	0–19	20–39	40–59	60–79	80–100	Total	
Under $1,000...............	88	4		2	6	100	51
$1,000–$4,999..............	69	8	6	6	11	100	72
$5,000–$9,999..............	49	14	8	4	25	100	51
$10,000–$24,999............	37	11	8	16	28	100	74
$25,000–$49,999............	9	9	18	24	39	99[a]	33
$50,000–$99,999............	6	17		11	67	101[a]	18
$100,000 and over..........			10	4	87	101[a]	31
	46	9	7	9	29	100	330

[a] Does not add to 100 percent because of rounding.

SUs fall in this category when equities in the SUs' residences and checking account balances are excluded from the measure. However, both tables show that the variable-dollar composition of the portfolio varies directly with the total assets of the SU.

Income is also an index of financial ability. Thus, a direct relationship between this variable and variable-dollar composition is to be expected. Cross-classification tables of income, V, and V^* show relationships which are similar to, although less pronounced than, those shown in Tables 8 and 9.

A third, and in some ways more reasonable, hypothesis relating financial ability to portfolio composition can be stated in terms of the interaction between savings and income. For example, if total savings are small but income is relatively high, as is frequently the case with young SUs, and if total savings are relatively large and income relatively low, as is the case with SUs who have sizable inheritances and older SUs, an interaction term such as savings times income may be more closely related to variable-dollar composition than either income or total savings. Each of these hypotheses will be tested in the following analysis.[66]

Although factors which relate to the financial requirements of the SU are more difficult to obtain, two nonfinancial variables which are available (age and SU size) may have some of the desired characteristics, i.e., different financial needs may be associated with SUs of different sizes and ages.

A priori reasoning leads one to expect a curvilinear effect, particularly in the age-V^* relationship. For example, young SUs with small children could be expected to hold the majority of their assets in fixed-dollar form because of their pronounced need for an emergency fund and the fact that they have had a relatively short period of time in which to accumulate a sizable amount of savings.[67] The oldest SUs could also be expected to hold large fixed-dollar components because of more frequent illnesses and the fact that they may be more dependent on their savings and the income derived therefrom for day-to-day living expenses. The middle-aged group of SUs should be affected less by these factors and may hold larger variable-dollar components than do SUs in the extreme age groups.

The effect of age on the distribution of V is more difficult to specify. It may be that younger SUs' equities in their homes represent the larger part of their savings; hence they may have predominantly variable-dollar portfolios when their total assets are considered. Furthermore, the fact that the oldest SUs have had more time to accumulate equity in their homes, as well as other funds, may mean that they are better able to accept the risks of holding predominantly variable-dollar assets.

Cross-classification tables of age and portfolio composition do not reveal marked patterns to support these hypotheses. However, when the influence of financial ability is held constant, as it is in the multiple regression computations, the age variable may be a significant factor.

As with the age variable, it is difficult to specify the effect of the size of the SU on portfolio composition because of possible counterbalancing

---

[66] The availability of credit is also one aspect of the financial ability of an SU. However, it is highly correlated with the net worth of the SU and an independent index of credit rating of the vast majority of the SUs is virtually impossible to obtain.

[67] Young SUs without children may have slightly higher variable-dollar ratios; however, there are few young SUs in the sample who do not have children.

factors. For example, as size increases greater demands are made on both income and savings for current consumption expenditures. This tends to reduce the amount of funds available for investment. There is also a need for a larger liquid emergency fund the more members there are in the SU. But offsetting this factor, there is need for larger homes which may result in relatively larger investment in housing. Hence, the two effects may offset each other in the distribution of V. Additional complications may be present because young one- and two-person SUs have relatively less need for emergency funds than do older SUs of the same size.

As in the case of variables representing financial ability, it is possible that a composite variable representing financial demands placed on the SU may be more efficient in the explanation of portfolio composition than each of the variables taken individually. Such a variable is difficult to define operationally. A set of modified life-cycle variables or a quantitative interaction variable such as age times family size could be used. While the latter variable represents an unusual mixing of dimensions, its use is defensible if it does represent an underlying continuum of financial demands placed on the SU such that at low values of the variable there is relatively less need for funds for current consumption and liquid assets than there is at high values of the variable.

Nonfinancial Factors

Throughout the study emphasis has been placed on the importance of psychological factors in the determination of portfolio composition. If the SU has adequate savings, a priori reasoning leads one to expect factors such as individual personality differences, motives for saving, expectations about economic conditions and prices, attitudes toward risk, and perceptions of assets to be important variables. Fortunately, in the course of the work of the Consumer Savings Project, information about most of these variables is being collected for at least part of the sample. Although the necessity of obtaining information for a wide variety of methodological experiments precluded the possibility of obtaining complete information on all of the psychological variables for the total sample, all of the SUs were asked to give their motives for saving; and personality tests,[68] attitudes about past economic and price conditions, and expectations of future economic and price conditions were obtained for a large part of the sample used in this study.

---

[68] Edwards Personal Preference Schedules were administered to the sample in one of the cities covered. The test is a well-accepted means of measuring several *normal* personality traits. For a more complete discussion, see Allen L. Edwards, *Edwards Personal Preference Schedule: Manual* (New York: Psychological Corporation, 1959).

It is difficult to predict a priori the effects of the various motives for saving on portfolio composition because of differences in the relative strengths of the motives and the interactions of the motives and other factors. The same is true of the characteristics measured in the personality tests. However, the relationships between the dependent variables and the expectation variables are easier to hypothesize. Since the portfolio an SU holds at any given time may be a result of past conditions as well as future expectations, both time dimensions may be important. SUs who expected prosperity in the past and expect it in the future can be expected to hold higher proportions of their savings in variable-dollar assets than those who held, and now hold, contrary opinions. The same should be true of SUs who expected in the past, or now expect, inflation in prices as contrasted to those who expected, or now expect, the general level of prices to decline.

Cross-classification tables of the expectation variables and the dependent variables show few differences in the portfolio composition for those who hold opposite opinions; however, the real test of the usefulness of such tables depends on their net contribution when the influence of the other variables is held constant.

A direct relationship between the education level of the head of the SU and the proportion of the portfolio held in variable-dollar assets is to be expected. However, it is difficult to obtain the appropriate education variable for inclusion in the model. It is likely that years of formal education is not the relevant variable and that some measure of the degree of economic or financial awareness is needed, for as was pointed out earlier, the variable-dollar assets are more difficult to acquire and require a greater degree of financial sophistication for efficient management. Since no measure of financial or economic education is available, years of formal education must be used as a rough index of the appropriate variable. This index may not be too far off since the more formal education one has, the greater opportunity he has to become acquainted with the more complex assets and the processes of investing in them.

Although the occupation of the head of the SU may be correlated with the financial ability of the SU as measured by income, it may exert an independent effect on portfolio composition. For example, self-employed SUs could be expected to have larger proportions of their savings in variable-dollar assets than SUs engaged in other occupations. Also, individuals employed in business-oriented jobs may be more likely to invest in variable-dollar assets because of a greater degree of familiarity with business and financial conditions. On the other hand, those employed as sales or clerical personnel or as skilled or unskilled laborers are less likely to be exposed to variable-dollar assets in the course of their work and, as a consequence, may be less likely to consider them as desirable investments.

Specification of the Variables

The foregoing preliminary analysis and a priori reasoning indicates that there is little reason to expect clear, simple relationships between the dependent and independent variables. For this reason, in the following analysis several alternative specifications of the variables are tested in the regressions. For example, where it is consistent with a priori reasoning, logarithmic, logistic, or dummy variable transformations are made and substituted for the linear form of the variables.

The use of the dummy variable technique offers two distinct advantages.[69] First, the technique provides a way to include variables which are ordinarily considered as non-quantifiable. Variables such as occupation, motives for saving, and membership in a certain class (such as being a home owner, or a non-home owner) are not based on an underlying quantifiable continuum. Through the use of the dummy variable technique this obstacle can be overcome and these variables can be included in an ordinary regression analysis.

Second, dummy variables can be used to good advantage where there may be a curvilinear relation between the conventionally scaled continuous variable and the dependent variable, but the relationship is difficult to specify a priori. In this case, the parameters of the set of dummy variables which is used to replace the continuous variable will reflect the curvilinear relationship.

In either case, whether the underlying variable is quantifiable or not, the method of using dummy variables is the same. A separate dummy variable is specified for each class in which the sample item may occur. For example, if there are five occupational classes, the variable representing the occupation of the sample item is designated by some constant (e.g., +1) and the other four variables receive a zero observation. In order to avoid the problem of over-identification which is created by the perfect negative correlation between the mutually exclusive set of dummy variables, a constraint must be placed on the system. One such constraint is to drop one of the dummy variables from each mutually exclusive system. For example, any one of the five occupational variables could be omitted from the actual computations. The remaining variables would no longer be perfectly correlated and the solution for the parameters would be determinant.

---

[69] For a more complete discussion of this technique, see Daniel B. Suits, "Use of Dummy Variables in Regression Equations," *Journal of the American Statistical Association,* Vol. 52, No. 280 (December, 1957), pp. 548-51.

A total of 49 separate independent variables was used at various points in the analysis. In all cases where the dummy variable technique required the omission of a variable, the "not ascertained" variable was dropped. The following list gives the number and description of each of the variables used.

List of the Variables Used

Designation   *Description*

X_1 = The percentage of total savings held in variable-dollar assets

X_{1a} = The percentage of discretionary savings held in variable-dollar assets

X_2 = Total assets (alternatively specified in actual amounts, logarithmic form, and logistic form)

X_{2a} = Total discretionary assets (alternatively specified in actual amounts, logarithmic form, and logistic form)

X_3 = Index of financial ability (income times assets)

X_{3a} = Index of financial ability (income times discretionary assets)

X_4 = Index of financial needs (age times number of persons in the SU)

X_5 = Number of persons in the SU

X_6 = Years of formal education of the head of the SU (as a continuous variable)

X_7 = Less than 12 years of formal education

X_8 = 12 to 15 years of formal education

X_9 = 16 or more years of formal education

X_{10} = Years of formal education not ascertained

X_{11} = Age of the head of the SU (as a continuous variable)

X_{12} = Less than 40 years of age

X_{13} = 40 to 49 years of age

X_{14} = 50 to 59 years of age

X_{15} = 60 or more years of age

X_{16} = Age not ascertained

X_{17} = Professional or manager working for others

X_{18} = Self-employed professional or proprietor

X_{19} = Clerical or sales

X_{20} = Skilled or unskilled labor

X_{21} = Retired

X_{22} = Occupation not ascertained

X_{23} = Total 1959 income

X_{24} = Home ownership

X_{25} = Expected prosperity during last 10 years

X_{26} = Expected recession during last 10 years

Designation   *Description*

X_{27} = Past economic expectations not ascertained

X_{28} = Expect prosperity in the future

X_{29} = Expect recession in the future

X_{30} = Future economic expectations not ascertained

X_{31} = Expected inflation in the past 10 years

X_{32} = Expected general fall in prices in past 10 years

X_{33} = Expected prices to remain stable in past 10 years

X_{34} = Past price expectations not ascertained

X_{35} = Expect inflation in the future

X_{36} = Expect general fall in prices in the future

X_{37} = Expect prices to remain stable in the future

X_{38} = Future price expectations not ascertained

X_{39} = Saving for old age

X_{40} = Saving for inheritance for children

X_{41} = Saving for education for children

X_{42} = Saving to pay off debt

X_{43} = Saving for major purchase

X_{44} = Saving for an emergency

X_{45} = Short-term saving motives (components of $X_{39, \ 41, \ 42, \ 43}$ and X_{11})

X_{46} = Achievement score

X_{47} = Change score

V. RESULTS AND CONCLUSIONS

Two approaches to the analysis were taken. In the first, regression equations were specified and computed using the observations of the total sample. At various stages of the analysis each of the listed variables was brought into the equations.

In the second approach the sample was stratified by three different independent variables in an attempt to find homogeneous subgroups of the total sample. This stratification was carried out successively since the size of the sample precluded the use of more than one variable at a time. Separate regressions using the variables listed earlier were run on each of the following strata:

(1) less than $10,000 in total assets,
(2) $10,000 to $24,999 in total assets,
(3) under $25,000 in total assets (strata 1 and 2 combined),
(4) $25,000 or more in total assets,
(5) home owners,
(6) non-home owners,
(7) business owners, and
(8) non-business owners.

In evaluating the results of the regressions the following criteria were used:

(1) the statistical significance of the regression coefficients,
(2) the stability of the regression coefficients when variables were deleted or added to the function,
(3) the proportion of the variation of the dependent variable accounted for, and
(4) the reasonableness of the results.

In the following section summary tables are presented for only the most successful models. However, as each part of the results is presented, possible alternative explanations are investigated and negative results obtained in ineffectual attempts are discussed.

71

The Results

The best results, according to the criteria outlined, were obtained when the total sample was stratified by home ownership. Stratification by business ownership produced virtually the same results for the owner and nonowner strata as those found for the total sample. Stratification by the amount of savings of the SU produced lower coefficients of multiple determination and fewer significant regression coefficients than were obtained in the analysis by home ownership. In addition, this analysis

TABLE 10. COEFFICIENTS OF NET REGRESSION FOR SELECTED
INDEPENDENT VARIABLES AND COEFFICIENTS OF MULTIPLE
DETERMINATION OBTAINED IN THE ANALYSIS
OF THE TOTAL PORTFOLIO

Variable (1)	Net regression coefficients			
	Home owners (N=253) (2)	Non-home owners (N=44) (3)	Total sample (N=297) (4)	Subsample (N=104) (5)
Total assets..............	2.79[a] (.96)	7.25[a] (2.63)	12.12[a] (1.27)	12.60[a] (2.32)
Income..............	1.45 (1.85)	5.72 (7.10)	−4.32 (2.23)	7.15 (4.05)
Age.................	− .44[a] (.11)	.44 (.47)	− .68[a] (.16)	− .70[a] (.28)
SU size..............	2.64[a] (.97)	−3.24 (3.02)	2.88[b] (1.29)	2.67 (1.91)
Self-employed[c].........		44.81[b] (20.41)	.78 (4.11)	6.06 (6.67)
Saving for purchase.....	−6.99[a] (2.67)	13.15 (9.72)	−8.89[a] (3.42)	−12.39[b] (5.61)
Expect prosperity[d]......				−9.72 (6.54)
Expect recession[d].......				−1.32 (8.05)
Expect price rise[d].......				8.92 (6.18)
Expect price decline[d]....				−12.80 (15.92)
Achievement score[d].....				.36 (.64)
Change score[d].........				.43 (.47)
Multiple determination coefficients............	.188[a]	.564[a]	.367[a]	.376[a]

a Statistically significant at the .01 level.
b Statistically significant at the .05 level.
c Omitted from the home owner stratum.
d Available for only 104 SUs.

Table 11. Coefficients of Net Regression for Selected
Independent Variables and Coefficients of Multiple
Determination Obtained in the Analysis
of the Discretionary Portfolio

Variable (1)	Net regression coefficients			
	Home owners (N=253) (2)	Non-home owners (N=44) (3)	Total sample (N=297) (4)	Subsample (N=104) (5)
Total assets..............	10.73[a] (1.30)	6.24[b] (2.62)	10.23[a] (1.15)	8.47[a] (2.17)
Income..............	6.45[b] (2.99)	6.09 (7.98)	7.12[a] (2.72)	8.99 (4.74)
Age.................	−.66[a] (.22)	.48 (.53)	−.50[b] (.20)	.34 (.31)
SU size.............	.43 (1.89)	−4.50 (3.37)	−.23 (1.61)	.79 (1.70)
Self-employed.........	16.85[a] (5.40)	42.95 (22.78)	19.26[a] (5.16)	34.60[a] (7.49)
Saving for purchase.....	−7.19 (4.73)	15.40 (10.82)	−5.17 (4.25)	−9.01 (6.30)
Expect prosperity[c]......				−.51 (7.28)
Expect recession[c].......				4.18 (8.91)
Expect price rise[c].......				.90 (6.82)
Expect price decline[c]....				7.97 (17.82)
Achievement score[c].....				−.90 (.72)
Change score[c].........				.70 (.53)
Multiple determination coefficients............	.513[a]	.529[a]	.506[a]	.528[a]

[a] Statistically significant at the .01 level.
[b] Statistically significant at the .05 level.
[c] Available for only 104 SUs.

produced additional evidence that the home ownership stratification was
the most advantageous in lieu of simultaneous stratification.

Table 10 summarizes the results of the regressions used to explain
the variation in the composition of the total portfolio (V). Table 11 is
a similar summary of the results obtained in the analysis of the discretionary portfolio. To facilitate comparisons, the results obtained in the
analysis of the two home owner strata, of the total sample, and of the
subsample for which additional psychological data were available are
included in each of the tables.

Home Ownership

The data presented in Tables 10 and 11 indicate that the ownership or nonownership of a home has an important impact on the SU's portfolio composition. For example, slightly over one-third of the variance of V is accounted for when the regression function is fitted to observations for the total sample. When the sample is stratified by home ownership, however, the value of R^2 decreases by approximately 50 percent for the home owner stratum and increases by approximately the same amount for the nonowner stratum.

The values of the regression coefficients shown in columns 2 and 3 of Table 10 also suggest that there may be important differences in the influence of the independent variables in the two strata. For example, column 2 of Table 10 shows that a 1 percent increase in total assets is associated with a 2.79 percent increase in V in the home owner group, whereas column 3 of Table 10 shows that a similar increase in total assets is associated with a 7.25 percent increase in the dependent variable (V) in the renter stratum. In addition, significant negative coefficients for the age and saving-for-purchase variables and a significant positive coefficient for the size of the SU variable are shown in the home owner stratum but not in the renter stratum. Also, the self-employed occupation variable failed to be significant and showed strong evidence of multicollinearity with total assets in the home owner stratum, whereas in the non-home owner group, no evidence of multicollinearity between total assets and the self-employed variable was present and the regression coefficient for the latter was statistically significant.

Since the equity in the SU's home is one of the variable-dollar assets entering the computation of V and total assets, it is difficult to say whether the differences just enumerated represent differences in the influence of the variables on total portfolio behavior or simply the effect of home equity on the variable-dollar ratio in one group and not the other. Comparison of the results obtained in the analysis of V^* (where equity in homes is excluded) provides a partial answer to this question.

As might be expected, the differences between the two strata (as shown in Table 11) are more subtle than those found in the analysis of V. Table 11 shows that the proportion of the explained variation of V^* increases only slightly when the sample is stratified by home ownership. Some differences, although less pronounced than those discussed earlier, do occur in the size and significance of the regression coefficients obtained in the two strata. In the owner stratum significant coefficients are found for total discretionary assets, age, income, and the self-employed variable; in the nonowner stratum only total discretionary assets and the self-employed variable have significant regression coefficients. (Actually the coefficient for the self-employed variable is significant at the .06 level).

A third test of the real meaning of the differences in the results for the two strata can be made by investigation of the raw data. For example, if the SUs in the two strata are markedly different on other dimensions, then the results may reflect the differential effects of these variables rather than the effect of ownership or nonownership of a home.

Analysis of the various independent variables reveals that stratification by home ownership tends to have the effect of stratification by financial ability. For example, the mean values of total assets, total discretionary assets, income, V, and V^* are all significantly higher in the owner stratum than in the nonowner stratum. Hence, the differences in the regressions for the two strata may be attributable to differences in financial ability as well as to home ownership.

Unfortunately, the correlation between home ownership and asset level precludes the use of both as independent variables and the sample size is too small to permit stratification of the type necessary to separate the effects of home ownership and asset level more precisely (i.e., stratification of the home owner and the nonowner groups by asset level). However, simple stratification by asset level does give some additional information about the nature of impact of home ownership on portfolio composition. For example, the dummy variable for home ownership is the only variable with a significant regression coefficient in the analysis of the total portfolios of SUs with less than $25,000 in total assets. But home ownership fails to have a significant relationship to V in the "$25,000 or more" asset range. It also fails to have stable, significant regression coefficients in the analysis of the discretionary portfolio. These results show that home ownership has a greater impact on the total portfolios of SUs with small savings than on those with large savings and that the discretionary portfolios of both asset groups are relatively unaffected by home ownership. (The coefficients of multiple determination were generally about one-half as large in the asset strata as those found in the home ownership analysis.)

In view of the correlation between home ownership and asset level, the differential sensitivities of V and V^* to the independent variables are related to both factors in the following discussions.

Financial Variables

In general, the results obtained in the regressions support the hypotheses advanced in Chapter IV about the nature of the influence of the financial variables on portfolio composition.

Assets

Tables 10 and 11 show a significant positive relationship between the

TABLE 12. STANDARDIZED REGRESSION COEFFICIENTS FOR SELECTED
INDEPENDENT VARIABLES OBTAINED IN THE ANALYSIS
OF THE TOTAL PORTFOLIO

Variable	Standardized regression coefficients			
	Home owners	Non-home owners	Total sample	Subsample
Total assets...........	.1709[a]	.4598[a]	.6185[a]	.5688[a]
Income..............	.0671	.1294	−.1289	.1909
Age.................	−.2785[a]	.1842	−.2842[a]	−.2899[a]
SU size..............	.1871[a]	−.1453	.1355[b]	.1581
Self-employed[c]........		.2974[b]	.0101	.0798
Saving for purchase.....	−.1586[a]	.2040	−.1348[a]	−.2086[a]
Expect prosperity[d].....				−.1676
Expect recession[d]......				−.0181
Expect price rise[d]......				.1339
Expect price decline[d]....				.0763
Achievement score[d].....				.0481
Change score[d].........				.0762

[a] Statistically significant at the .01 level.
[b] Statistically significant at the .05 level.
[c] Available for only 104 SUs.
[d] Omitted from the home owner stratum.

log of total assets and V, and between the log of discretionary assets and
V^*, in both the home owner and non-home owner categories.[70] However,
as noted earlier, the amount of savings held does not appear to have the
same influence on home owners and non-home owners in the determination of the composition of their portfolios. For example, the measure of
variable-dollar composition of the total portfolio appears to be much
more sensitive to total assets in the nonowner group than in the owner
group. The reverse situation is true in the measurement of the variable-
dollar composition of the discretionary portfolio, i.e., a 1 percent increase
in total discretionary savings is associated with a 10.7 percent increase in
V^* for home owners and a 6.2 percent increase in V^* for non-owners.
The standardized regression coefficients (beta coefficients) also reflect
the differential influence of assets in the home owner and nonowner
strata. In every case but the total portfolios of home owners, the beta
coefficient for the asset variable is larger than that of any other variable
(Tables 12 and 13), thus indicating that the asset variable is the dominant

[70] Significant coefficients are also found for assets when specified in absolute
values. However, the over-all results of this analysis are far less satisfactory than
those obtained using the log transformation. The logarithmic transformation
amounts to an assumption that a constant rate of increase in assets is linearly
associated with a unit increase in the dependent variable, i.e., that a given absolute
increment to assets has relatively less effect on portfolio composition in the upper
range of the asset distribution than it has in the lower range.

Table 13. Standardized Regression Coefficients for Selected Independent Variables Obtained in the Analysis of the Discretionary Portfolio

Variable	Standardized regression coefficients			
	Home owners	Non-home owners	Total sample	Subsample
Total assets............	.5004[a]	.4008[b]	.4986[a]	.3822[a]
Income...............	.1371[b]	.1288	.1517[a]	.1875
Age..................	−.1920[a]	.1849	−.1489[b]	.1099
SU size...............	.0139	−.1886	−.0083	.0283
Self-employed.........	.1613[a]	.2665	.1780[a]	.3564[a]
Saving for purchase.....	−.0749	.2234	−.0559	−.1186
Expect prosperity[c]......				−.0069
Expect recession[c].......				.0450
Expect price rise[c].......				.0105
Expect price decline[c]....				.0372
Achievement score[c].....				.0954
Change score[c].........				.0972

[a] Statistically significant at the .01 level.
[b] Statistically significant at the .05 level.
[c] Omitted from the home owner stratum.

variable in all of the regressions except the regression of V in the home owner group.

It is likely that these results are attributable to the effect of home ownership. For example, if there is a marked difference between the sensitivity of equity in homes and the sensitivity of other variable-dollar holdings to the amount of savings an SU has, one would expect to find the results shown here. That is, in the analysis of the variable-dollar composition of the total portfolio one would expect the regression coefficient for total assets to be significantly lower for home owners than for non-home owners because of the influence of home equity. On the other hand, in the analysis of the discretionary portfolio in the home owner stratum (where the equity in homes is excluded from the measure of composition and from the amount of assets), one would expect the regression coefficient for assets to be higher than that found in the analysis of the total portfolio. Further evidence supporting this explanation is shown in the stability of the regression coefficient for V and total assets and for V^* and total discretionary assets in the analysis of the nonowner stratum.

In a further attempt to obtain the best estimate of the relationship of asset level on portfolio composition, logistic transformations of total assets and discretionary assets were substituted into the model for the logarithmic specifications.[71] Although this attempt did produce significant coefficients for the asset variables, R^2 was much smaller in every case and the over-all results suggested that logarithmic specification was best.

Income

The results shown in Tables 10 and 11 indicate that income has relatively little influence on the proportion of assets held in variable-dollar form. The regression coefficient for the log of income failed to be significantly different from zero in any of the analyses of the total portfolio. Although income is significant in the analysis of the discretionary portfolio (a 1 percent increase in income is associated with a 6.5 percent increase in V^* in the home owner stratum), analysis of the beta coefficients for this stratum reveals that income is considerably less important than discretionary assets and slightly less important than age in explaining variation in V^*. (Specification of income in absolute values failed to produce significant coefficients in any of the analyses.)

Interaction Variables

In Chapter IV hypotheses were presented which suggested that portfolio composition might be more closely related to interaction variables representing aggregate financial ability or to the difference between such an interaction variable and an index of financial needs. At one stage of the analysis, composite variables utilizing assets, income, age, and SU size were computed and substituted in the model for the individual variables. The interaction variables were statistically significant in nearly every case, but they produced coefficients of multiple determination which were much lower than those obtained when the variables were specified individually.

Nonfinancial Variables

Age

The data in Table 10 show that a 10-year increase in the age of the head of the SU is associated with a 4.4 percent decrease in the value of V in the home owner stratum. This regression coefficient is significant at the .01 probability level. However, the regression coefficient estimating the relationship between age and V in the nonowner stratum is not significantly different from zero. Similarly, the results shown in Table 11 indicate that an increase of 10 years in the age of the head of the SU is

---

[71] Use of the logistic transformation is not inconsistent with a priori reasoning about the effect of assets of portfolio composition. It amounts to an assumption that increases in assets have relatively less effect on the variable-dollar ratio in the two extremes of the asset distribution than it has in the middle range. Thus, the assumption is that the relationship is best described by a growth curve, i.e., a function which looks like an elongated S.

associated with a 6.6 percent decrease in the value of V^*. This coefficient is also significant at the .01 probability level. As in the analysis of V, however, the regression coefficient for age and V^* is not significantly different from zero for the nonowner group.

These results suggest that age exerts a significant negative influence on portfolio composition in the group of home owners but that in the nonowner group this influence of age is not present, or at least is not ascertainable in this sample.

The nonsignificance of this variable in the nonowner stratum is inconsistent with the assumed effect of age on portfolio composition. Examination of the age distributions of the two strata showed them to be remarkably similar — the mean age and standard deviation of the owner group are 47.7 and 12.0 years respectively, and the mean age and standard deviation of the nonowner group are 47.8 and 12.18 respectively. Hence the differences could not be attributed to this factor.

Investigation of the zero-order correlation coefficient between age and the other variables also failed to produce information which could be used to explain the differences.

The explanation of these differences appears to be in interactions of age and other variables in the two strata. Although the net regression coefficients represent the *net* effect of a given variable when the influence of other specified variables is held constant, there is some evidence that the differences in financial ability between the two strata account for the differential effects of age. For example, when the sample was stratified by total assets the regression coefficient for age was significantly negative for the group having over $25,000 in total assets. However, the coefficient was not significantly different from zero for the group with less than $25,000 in assets. Similar results were found in the analysis of both V and V^*. This suggests that the lack of funds acts as a constraint on variation in portfolio composition at lower levels of financial ability and that other factors play a measurable part only at the higher levels of financial ability where adequate funds are available. Since stratification by home ownership tends to have the same effect as stratification by asset level, the differences in the effect of age in the two ownership strata may be another reflection of the difference in financial ability.

Specification of age as a system of dummy variables did not produce signs of marked curvilinearity or improvements in the results over those obtained when age was specified as a continuous variable.

Size of SU

Contrary to a priori expectations, the number of persons in the SU does not appear to have a negative effect on the proportion of assets held in variable-dollar form. Table 10 shows that in the home owner stratum an increase of 2.6 percent in V is associated with each increase in the number of persons in the SU. In addition, Table 11 shows that in the same stratum, when equity in homes is excluded from the measures of variable-dollar composition and assets, the regression coefficient for size of SU is not significantly different from zero. These results clearly contradict the hypothesis presented in Chapter IV, i.e., that increasing the size of the SU should have a negative effect on the variable-dollar ratio because of the greater needs for funds for current consumption and liquid reserves. It seems very likely that the significantly positive value of the coefficient in Table 10 and the nonsignificant value in Table 11 may indicate that larger savings units need larger, more expensive homes and as a consequence have relatively greater variable-dollar holdings in this form than do smaller SUs.

Occupation

Of the five occupation variables included in the analysis, only the dummy variable for the self-employed group appears to be significantly related to the variable-dollar ratios. Since business equity is one of the variable-dollar assets included in the computation of V and V^*, the significant positive association between these dependent variables and the self-employed variable is not surprising.

The results also reveal that the self-employed variable has a relatively greater effect on variable-dollar composition in the nonowner stratum than in the home owner stratum. Investigation of the zero-order correlation coefficients indicates that this result is not a reflection of a close association between the self-employed variable and assets and income. (The simple correlation coefficients between self-employed and assets and self-employed and income in the nonowner stratum are .20 and .02 respectively.) The only evidence of strong multicollinearity between the self-employed variable and the financial variables was the relationship between total assets and self-employed status in the analysis of the total portfolios of home owners.

The explanation of the differences in the regression coefficients appears to lie in the relative importance of business equity to SUs in the two strata. That is, since the non-home owner group tends to have lower asset holdings than the owner group, the holdings of the former are more likely to be highly concentrated in fewer assets. In the case of business ownership the concentration should be especially pronounced for this asset undoubtedly represents the SU's major source of income.

Motives for Saving

It is evident from the results presented in Tables 10 and 11 that the motive of saving for a purchase has a significant negative effect on the variable-dollar composition of the total portfolios of SUs who own their own homes. However, this variable apparently does not have a significant effect on the portfolio composition of non-home owners or on the composition of V^* for home owners. It is likely that the significance of this variable in the analysis of V and not of V^* is attributable to the exclusion of checking account balances from the latter measure. For example, if those who are saving to make some major purchase hold the funds in checking accounts rather than other assets, the exclusion of checking account balances from the measure of portfolio composition would necessarily reduce the significance of the motive as an explanatory variable.

The nonsignificance of the saving for purchase motive in the analysis of the non-home owners is not surprising. As pointed out earlier, these SUs tend to have lower financial assets and lower variable-dollar components in their portfolios than do the SUs who own their own homes. Thus, the inclusion of a motive which is associated with fixed-dollar assets is unlikely to make a significant net contribution to the explanation of portfolios which are already highly concentrated in fixed-dollar assets because of financial restrictions.

The regression coefficients for the other five motives for saving ($X_{40-43,45}$ in the list of variables) failed to be significantly different from zero in any of the regressions run on the total sample and the home ownership strata. Insignificant regression coefficients were also obtained for a composite variable representing short-term saving motives.[72]

Expectations and Personality Test Scores

Personality test scores and data on expectations of economic and price conditions were not available for the total sample. However, so long as no stratification was attempted enough data were available to permit a preliminary analysis of the effect of these variables on portfolio composition for a subsection of the total sample. Column 5 of Tables 10 and 11 shows the results of this analysis.

Examination of Tables 10 and 11 shows that the results obtained for

---

[72] In this attempt to ascertain the effect of motives for saving on portfolio composition it was reasoned that if the SUs were saving for some near-term goal the funds would more likely be held in fixed-dollar assets than if they were saving for a distant goal. Hence, a negative correlation between short-term motives and the variable-dollar ratios could be expected. In constructing this dummy variable the following SUs were given an observation of $+1$ and other SUs received a zero observation:

(1) SUs who were saving for a purchase, or to pay off debt;

(2) SUs who were saving for education of children and who had main wage-earners over 40 years of age; and

(3) SUs who were saving for old age and who had main wage-earners over 60 years of age.

the subsample and for the total sample are very similar on all of the comparable items. Inclusion of the expectation variables and the personality variables assumed to be most important failed to produce a measurable improvement in the model. Moreover, none of the expectation and personality variables had a significant regression coefficient at the .05 level.[73]

The lack of significance of the expectation variables is consistent with the results found in the 1960 SCF and in the stock ownership study by Kreinin. That is, contrary to a priori reasoning, people who expect inflation do not hold more "inflation proof" portfolios than those who expect a stable price level.[74]

The lack of significance of the achievement variable (the need to do one's best, to accomplish significant results, to do a job well) does not appear to be consistent with Kreinin's stock ownership study where he found "accomplishment minded" individuals more prone to hold stocks.

Conclusions

In the following section both positive and negative conclusions which deal with the nature of the influence of the independent variables on portfolio composition are presented and discussed.

Home ownership and factors associated with home ownership have an important impact on the composition of SUs' portfolios.

Strong evidence to support this conclusion was found in the results shown in Tables 10 and 11 and in the results obtained when home ownership was specified as a dummy variable. These results indicated that home ownership strongly influences the composition of the total portfolio and the nature of the influence of other independent variables on total portfolio composition. The results also suggested that the models used here are least successful in explaining variation in the measure of portfolio composition which is most sensitive to equity in homes, i.e., V.

These results are not difficult to explain. For example, although the acquisition of a home undoubtedly represents the largest single commitment of funds most of the SUs will ever make, the decision to purchase a home is subject to strong emotional forces such as the need for security, prestige, and status. In addition, ownership of a home is an important determinant of the SUs' mode or way of life. Moreover, the asset characteristics of a residence are also unusual. The vast majority of the SUs do not own their homes free and clear of mortgages. The existence of a

---

[73] Recalled expectations about past price and economic conditions and other personality variables also failed to have significant regression coefficients.

[74] See Mordechai E. Kreinin, "Factors Associated with Stock Ownership," *loc. cit.*, and Survey Research Center, *1960 Survey of Consumer Finances*, p. 118.

mortgage means that consistent additions to their equity must be made. The contractual nature and the importance of this asset mean that even in times of financial stress SUs may have to acquire other debt to meet this obligation. Thus, the variable-dollar composition of their total portfolios may be increased in spite of the influence of other factors such as low asset level or low income.

No firm conclusions can be drawn about the impact of home ownership on the composition of the discretionary portfolio from the results presented in Tables 10 to 13. Although some differences in the regression coefficients did occur when the sample was stratified by home ownership, the proportion of the variance accounted for in the two strata was virtually unchanged by the stratification. In addition, when home ownership was treated as a dummy variable it failed to have stable, significant regression coefficients in the analyses of V^*. Detailed examination of the underlying data and alternative regressions suggests that the differences in the coefficients are most likely attributable to differentials in the financial ability of SUs in the two strata and to sampling errors.

The variable-dollar composition of portfolios is highly sensitive to the amount of savings held by the SU.

The results obtained in the analysis of the total sample, the subsample, and the two home owner strata all support this conclusion. In each of these analyses the regression coefficient for the amount of assets held by the SU was highly significant and, in all cases but one, the beta coefficients showed that this variable was relatively more important than any other. Thus, the analyses clearly support the hypotheses advanced in Chapter IV, i.e., that the amount of funds the SU has accumulated is a very important determinant of the variable-dollar ratio.

The results of the analyses also show that the relationship between the level of savings and the portfolio composition is not a simple one. Various approaches showed that significant regression coefficients could be obtained for the asset variable when it is specified in almost any form. However, the best results were obtained when a semilogarithmic function was used to describe the relationship. But even this specification did not result in a unique parameter which could be used to describe the sensitivity of the variable-dollar ratio to savings for all SUs.

The age of the head of the SU is negatively related to the variable-dollar composition of home owners' portfolios.

This conclusion confirms the hypothesis presented about the effect of advanced age on portfolio composition. That is, that older SUs tend to hold more conservative portfolios (higher concentrations of fixed-dollar assets) than do younger SUs.

The conclusion is also consistent with survey results obtained by Butters, Thompson, and Bollinger in their study of investments by individuals. That is, it was found that many elderly individuals with substantial savings indicated that they shifted funds from variable-dollar holdings to fixed-dollar form to meet future estate and inheritance taxes.[75] This factor (as well as the constraining effect of inadequate funds) may also help explain the nonsignificance of the age coefficient in the nonhome owner stratum, and the fact that age had a significant negative coefficient in the "$25,000 or more" stratum and not in the "under $25,000" savings stratum.

Income appears to have relatively little direct effect on portfolio composition.

Although income is obviously the major source of savings it is difficult to find statistical evidence that it exerts a pronounced independent effect on the proportion of savings held in variable form. The results did show a significant regression coefficient for income and V^* in the analysis of the total portfolio and in the home owner stratum. Even in these cases, however, the beta coefficients revealed that income makes a relatively unimportant contribution to the explained variance. Alternative specifications of income produced similar results.

It should be emphasized that one cannot infer from this conclusion that income has no effect whatsoever on portfolio composition. The results simply indicate that the effect of income as a single independent variable is not pronounced. It is still possible that it may make a significant contribution if properly specified in a complex interaction variable representing financial ability.

Only one occupational variable, self-employed, appears to have a significant influence on portfolio composition.

Surprisingly, belonging to an occupation group such as professional or manager working for others, clerical or sales, skilled or unskilled labor, or retired appears to have little or no effect on portfolio composition. Of all of the occupation variables used in the study, only the self-employed occupational variable was significantly related to the percentage of assets held in variable form. The significant, positive association between this variable and variable-dollar composition is to be expected since business equity is one of the variable-dollar assets included in the analysis. Although it is difficult to draw conclusions about the precise nature of the influence of being self-employed on portfolio composition, the results of the analysis of the stratification by home ownership and by asset levels indicated that the influence of this variable decreases as asset level rises and when home equity is included in the portfolio.

---

[75] Butters, Thompson, and Bollinger, *op. cit.*, p. 305.

The number of persons in the SU is positively associated with the proportion of total assets home owners hold in variable form.

Contrary to expectations of a significant negative effect of size of SU on the variable-dollar composition of the discretionary portfolio, the only significant coefficients for this variable were positive in sign and were found in the analysis of the total portfolio. Comparisons of the results of the various analyses suggest that the positive relationship between the size variable and *V* is attributable to the influence of equity in homes on the total portfolio and to the relative importance of this asset in the portfolios of large and small SUs.

Although the size of the SU undoubtedly exerts an indirect negative effect on portfolio composition through its influence on savings, the results of the regressions indicated that an independent, negative effect, if it exists, was not strong enough to be measured in this sample.

Only one motive, saving for a purchase, appears to have a measurable effect on the composition of the total portfolio.

Of the motives for saving which were included in the regression functions, only the motive of saving for a major purchase (over $100) proved to be significantly related to the dependent variable. The results showed that the existence of this motive has a negative influence on the variable-dollar ratio of the total portfolio. The absence of a measurable influence on the discretionary portfolio indicates that the majority of the earmarked funds must be held in checking accounts rather than in other fixed-dollar assets. Surprisingly, similar results were not found for the saving to pay off debt motive.

The absence of significant relationships between the other motives for saving and portfolio composition is more understandable. For example, the SU has a complex structure of motives for saving and any one of these motives may be related to several different assets. Thus, saving for old age for one SU may mean that part of its savings is held in savings accounts and is earmarked specifically for the SU's old age fund. But for a second SU, saving for old age may mean building up the equity in several pieces of property which will provide income in the future.

Psychological variables, such as expectations of prices and general economic conditions, and personality characteristics appear to have little influence on the variable-dollar ratio.

Since the real value of the SUs' savings depends in large part on the general economic and price conditions which prevail in the economy, one would expect the SUs' anticipations of these conditions to influence the way they hold their savings. However, the results clearly show that this is not the case. Of the 10 different expectational variables included in the analysis of a subsample of 104 SUs, not one proved to be significantly correlated with either of the dependent variables. This suggests either that the expectational variables exert no influence on portfolio composition or that the influence they do exert is totally obscured by other factors.

The same conclusion applies to the personality trait, "need for achievement," as measured by the tests administered to 104 SUs — that is, the trait does not materially influence portfolio selection or, if it does, its influence is not ascertainable in analysis of the variable-dollar composition.

In the case of the change variable the absence of significant relations may mean that the test did not isolate the relevant characteristics. For example, it was assumed that a willingness to undertake risks is significantly related to a high variable-dollar ratio and the "change" score was assumed to be the best available measure of this characteristic.[76] But the score on the change dimension of the test may not be an appropriate measure of this type of risk-taking. If this is the case, tests of alternative measures of willingness to take risks are clearly called for before final conclusions can be made.

The level of formal education of the head of the SU is unrelated to the composition of portfolios.

Contrary to a priori expectations, the years of formal education of the head of the SU failed to be significantly related to the dependent variables in any of the analyses undertaken.

As in the case of the personality variable "change," there is reason to believe that years of formal education is not the appropriate measure of the variable needed for this analysis. It was pointed out earlier that the variable-dollar assets were in many ways more complex than the fixed-dollar assets. As a result, SUs with greater financial knowledge and sophistication could be expected to concentrate more on variable-dollar assets than less well informed SUs. Since no measure of this type of knowledge was available, years of formal education was used as an approximation. Thus, the negative results obtained in the use of this variable do not necessarily invalidate the basic hypothesis.[77]

A cross-section analysis of the regression of variable-dollar ratios on the independent variables utilized in this study provides only a partial

---

[76] The change variable measures the need "to do new and different things . . . to experiment . . . to participate in new fads and fashions." Allen L. Edwards, *op. cit.,* p. 11.

[77] Information which could be used as a better indication of the SUs' knowledge of financial conditions were obtained on later reinterviews of part of the SUs included in this study. Although the data were obtained too late to be included in this analysis, they are being used in analyses currently being carried out by members of the Consumer Savings Project.

explanation of the variation in the variable-dollar composition of consumer savings portfolios.

Investigation of the coefficients of multiple determination shows that this negative conclusion is clearly warranted. Even the best of the models failed to account for more than 53 percent of the variation of the dependent variable. The rather low coefficients of determination may be due to the following reasons.

First, variables other than those available for use here may be important in the determination of portfolio composition. Some of these have been alluded to in the preceding pages; others are discussed in the development of hypotheses for future study.

Second, although the basic premise of the model developed in Part Two and used in Part Three is that the behavior of the individual is a function of all of the forces acting on the individual at that instant in time, the portfolio the individual holds may represent influences of the past as well as those now present. That is, the individual may now feel that a portfolio other than that which he presently holds is desirable, but he may be reluctant to change because of the costs of time, trouble, and money (e.g., possible losses of principal if the asset is sold, or possible taxes if there has been a capital gain, or commissions to be paid for buying and selling securities or real estate). Thus, there may be a good deal of inertia in changing the composition of accumulated savings and a cross-section analysis of portfolio composition and the present conditions may be, as a consequence, only partially successful.

The third reason is explained in the following tentative conclusion about the way consumers select assets.

In selecting a holding, consumers give primary consideration to the specific needs the holding satisfies and considerably less emphasis to the effect this holding has on portfolio composition.

The results of the regression analyses, as well as the analyses undertaken in Part Two, strongly suggest that consumers give little consideration to the problem of portfolio composition. That is, consumers have specific motives for acquiring a holding and rarely does the place this holding occupies in the total portfolio affect the decision to acquire the holding. This conclusion may not be equally applicable to consumers of all degrees of financial ability, but it is likely that it is most applicable to the majority of the SUs covered in this study.

Limitations

The limitations relating to the nature of the sample used, the time period, and geographic area covered which were discussed in Chapter III are equally applicable to the conclusions arrived at in Chapter V. In addition, there are limitations to the conclusions presented in Chapter V which are attributable to the nature of the results obtained in regression analyses.

Throughout the analysis attempts were made to specify models, consistent with a priori reasoning and the limitations of the data, which would produce stable, statistically significant regression coefficients and high coefficients of multiple determination. But even in cases of highly significant regression coefficients and coefficients of determination near 1.0, there is always the possibility that the covariation is spurious or caused by unspecified factors. Thus, in the final analysis, statistical significance does not *prove* causation. In view of this general limitation, the wide confidence intervals for many of the regression coefficients, the large part of the variation of the dependent variables left unexplained, and the possible atypical nature of the sample used in the analysis, the magnitudes of the regression coefficients and the conclusions based on them should be interpreted as first approximations of the underlying relationships which have yet to be subjected to tests of reliability and validity.

VI. SUMMARY AND HYPOTHESES FOR FUTURE STUDY

In the following pages a brief summary of the major findings of the study is presented and hypotheses for future study are discussed.

In the analysis of the asset composition of consumer savings port-folios, it was found that with relatively minor exceptions, the ownership of one holding, or combination of holdings, had no effect on the owner-ship of another holding, or combination of holdings. This lack of inter-action between assets was found for combinations of all sizes and for all strata of SUs. The major exceptions were significantly positive devia-tions for combinations of holdings which contain both stock and govern-ment bonds and significantly negative deviations for combinations which contain both businesses and pension plans. However, in combinations including all four holdings the difference between the actual value and the expected value was not significantly different from zero.

When the algebraic difference between the actual proportion and the expected proportion of the sample owning a certain combination was converted to a relative basis, it was found that the great majority of the independence estimates were within ±10 percent of the actual value. It was pointed out that these results may have important implications for financial institutions who deal in these holdings. If the institution knows how many people of a given area own individual holdings, they can pre-dict how many own, as well as how many do not own, various combina-tions of the holdings.

In Chapter III it was shown that the independence phenomenon does not necessarily mean that people fail to consider their present holdings when acquiring other assets, but that this result could easily be attributed to the complex structure of multiple motives for holding assets and the multidimensional nature of assets.

In Part Three, emphasis was placed on a different aspect of portfolio composition, i.e., the fixed- versus variable-dollar composition of con-sumer savings portfolios. The problem was cast in the conceptual frame-work developed in Part Two, and several multiple regression analyses, in which the composition of total portfolios and the composition of the discretionary portfolios were dependent variables, were carried out in an attempt to find the factors which explain the variation in the variable-dollar composition of portfolios.

The results of the regression analyses clearly demonstrated that home ownership and total assets were major determinants of the composition of the total portfolio. They also indicated that home owners' portfolios were more sensitive than nonowners' portfolios to variation in independent variables such as age, size of SU, and saving for purchase motive, and less sensitive to variables such as total assets and occupation.

The results of the analyses of the discretionary portfolio showed that this measure of variable-dollar composition was highly sensitive to discretionary assets but relatively insensitive to home ownership, SU size, and the saving for purchase motive.

Although there were indications that the nature of their effect was influenced by the level of the financial ability of the SUs, it was also shown that variables such as age, self-employed occupation, and income influenced the composition of the discretionary portfolio.

Contrary to a priori expectations, other motives for saving, past and present price and economic expectations, personality characteristics, years of formal education, and occupations other than self-employed failed to have significant regression coefficients in any of the analyses. The overall results of the regression analyses showed that even the best models failed to account for almost one-half of the variation of the dependent variables. These results, as well as the results obtained in Part Two, suggested a conclusion similar to that reached by Guthrie.[78] That is, the great majority of the SUs give far more consideration to the specific needs each asset fulfills than to the effect the asset has on the total portfolio. Limitations to the conclusion were pointed out in Chapters III and V.

In the introductory chapter, it was pointed out that this is an exploratory study of consumer savings portfolios. As such, one of the services the study should provide is a useful guide for future research. All of the conclusions arrived at here should be interpreted as first approximations in need of further confirmation. Future research designed specifically for analyses of portfolio composition should be able to provide this confirmation or refutation.

In particular, the independence hypothesis provides a provocative issue to be tested in future analyses. To provide a good test of the hypothesis, considerably larger samples are needed than were available for this study. Larger samples would allow more detailed analysis of

---

[78] See Harold W. Guthrie, "Consumers' Propensities to Hold Liquid Assets," *loc. cit.*

homogeneous socioeconomic groups, and the independence hypothesis could be extended and tested for broad asset groups such as fixed- and variable-dollar assets or liquid and nonliquid assets.[79] Also, in future studies direct questioning of SUs about the independence of holdings could be carried out.

Several hypotheses about factors which may be important in the fixed- versus variable-dollar composition of portfolios are suggested by the analyses carried out in Chapter IV. The results of these analyses point up the importance of samples large enough to allow stratification by home ownership and financial ability at the same time. With this research design separate regressions could be run on each of the strata and better estimates of the effects of the other independent variables could be made.

Larger samples are also needed to investigate the portfolio behavior of SUs with sizable holdings (e.g., over $100,000), for the results here indicate that the interaction of the variables is not the same at all asset levels.

Additional work on the interaction variables for financial ability and needs may provide interesting results. Although the measures used here produced significant regression coefficients of the right signs, alternative measures and specifications may produce significant improvements in the results. In particular, emphasis should be placed on the role of income in these interaction variables, since this analysis indicated that income specified as a single variable has relatively little influence on portfolio composition and a priori reasoning leads one to expect a strong relationship.

The results of the analysis carried out in Chapter IV also showed that the years of formal education the head of the SU had was not associated with the composition of the portfolio. However, it is possible that a measure of general financial or economic education could be devised which would prove to be associated with the proportion of assets held in variable dollars. Such a measure could be obtained by asking SUs a series of questions about interest rates on different assets, the effect of inflation and deflation on the value of certain assets, and current economic and financial conditions.

In future investigations attempts should also be made to obtain additional psychological variables to be used in the analysis. It is likely that alternative measures of personality traits such as the willingness to take risks and achievement need would produce improvements in the results.

In addition, direct questioning of SUs about the portfolio concept

---

[79] This was not possible in this study because of the nature of the sample design.

may produce information which would be of value to future analysis. For example, questions should be asked about consciousness of SUs of their over-all portfolio composition and its relevance to external financial and economic conditions, about their satisfaction with their current portfolio, and about the nature and amount of shifting of assets they do.

APPENDIXES

APPENDIX A: DERIVATION OF THE BEST ESTIMATE

Information obtained from cooperating financial institutions made possible the derivation of a "best estimate" of each SU's savings in two of the holdings.[80] The "best estimate," derived from both respondent and institution reports, was used throughout the entire analysis. A deviant case analysis was made of each respondent's report (R) which varied by more than ± 10 percent of the institution's report (I). The institution's report (I) was taken as the best estimate unless there was overwhelming objective evidence indicating that R was correct. For example, if R used records, gave exact dollar and cents amounts, was completely cooperative and interested in the study, or if the interviewer recorded the amounts directly from records, the amounts R reported were taken as the best estimate. However, in the great majority of the cases the amount reported by I was taken as the best estimate.

In order to determine the best estimate of each SU's total savings in each of the validated holdings, the following framework was used:

(A) Accurate report: $R = I$ for all validation items

(B) Validation item and balance reported: R deviates from I by more than ± 10 percent of I
  (1) Only validation item reported
  (2) Validation item plus other items reported
    (a) Deliberate error (e.g., R uncooperative, consistently understates amounts, refuses to use records)
    (b) Accidental error (e.g., owner not present in interview, R completely cooperative and gives accurate amounts on other holdings)

(C) Validation item reported: Amount not ascertained
  (1) Only validation item reported
  (2) Validation item plus same type of holding with noncooperating institution
    (a) Amounts given

---

[80] Best estimates for non-validated holdings were derived from consistency checks of all information given by the SU on previous interviews.

(b) Amounts not given

    (i) Similar item (e.g., both validated item and non-validated item belong to a child)

    (ii) Dissimilar item (e.g., validated item belongs to an adult and non-validated item belongs to a child)

(D) Validation item not reported

    (1) No similar items reported

    (2) Items similar to validation item reported

The correction procedure followed for each of the categories is as follows:

Category A: No correction necessary.

Category B1: The best estimate was used.

Category B2a: All items reported were corrected by the percentage error on the validating item.

Category B2b: The best estimate was used for the validated item only, no corrections made on other items.

Category C1: The amount reported by the institution was used as the best estimate.

Category C2a: No corrections were made on non-validated items.

Category C2bi: The mean value of validated items were taken as the best estimate of each of the non-validated items.

Category C2bii: The sample was first stratified by income and the mean value of similar items computed for each stratum. The mean value of the item for the SU's income stratum was used as the best estimate for each non-validated item reported with amount not ascertained. For example, if the non-validated item was a child's holding and the SU's income was between $5,000 and $7,499, then the mean value of all similar holdings belonging to children in SUs in the $5,000 to $7,499 income stratum was used as the best point estimate of the balance in the non-validated holding.

Category D1: The sample was stratified by income and age and the mean number of items computed for each stratum. The mean for the stratum in which the SU falls was used as the best estimate of the number of items owned. The mean value of all items reported by the institution was then multiplied by the mean number of accounts to get the best estimate of the theoretically non-reported amounts. This amount, added to the amount reported by the institution for the validation item, was taken as the best estimate of the total holdings.

Category D2: The best estimate for the validating item was added to the amounts in the items reported.

At the time this study was made, validation on one of the holdings had not been completed for one-half[81] of the SUs in one of the cities. The results of the completed validation indicated that the major bias in this holding was due to non-reporting rather than to underreporting. Consequently, an estimate of the non-reported holdings for the non-validated half was needed. Since the SUs selected for validation had been randomly chosen, for the purposes of this study it was assumed that the size distribution of non-reported holdings would be the same for both parts of the sample. Using this assumption, it was then possible to use the Monte Carlo technique to distribute the theoretically non-reported items to the individual SUs in the non-validated part of the sample. The procedure used was as follows: let

P_1 = number of items reported by only the institution for the validated part of the sample,

P_1^* = theoretical number of items reported only by the institution for the non-validated part of the sample,

P_R = total number of items reported by the SUs in the validated part of the sample, and

P_R^* = total number of items reported by the SUs in the nonvalidated part of the sample.

Then

(1)
$$\frac{P_I}{P_R + P_I} = \frac{P_I^*}{P_R^* + P_I^*}.$$

After solving equation (1) for P_I^*, a frequency distribution of the P_I^* items having the same mean and dispersion as the P_I items was created. Cross-classifications were then made of income and the size of the items for the entire sample. This gave the probability of an SU in a given income stratum owning an item of a given size. Then, using a table of random numbers and the probabilities determined above, all P_I^* items were distributed to SUs in the various income strata.

APPENDIX B: DERIVATION OF CONDITIONS 1, 2, AND 3

Conditions 1, 2, and 3 are obtained from equation (3.5) in the following manner:

(3.5)
$$[P(a_i) + P(a_j) - P(a_{ij})] [P(b_i) + P(b_j) - P(b_{ij})]$$
$$= P(a_ib_i) + P(a_ib_j) + P(a_jb_i) + P(a_jb_j) - P(a_ib_{ij})$$
$$- P(a_jb_{ij}) - P(a_{ij}b_i) - P(a_{ij}b_j) + P(a_{ij}b_{ij}).$$

---

[81] The non-validated SUs were approximately one-fourth of the total sample.

Multiplying the terms in the left side of 3.5 gives

$$(3.5a) \quad P(a_i) P(b_i) + P(a_i) P(b_j) + P(a_j) P(b_i) + P(a_j) P(b_j)$$
$$- P(a_i) P(b_{ij}) - P(a_j) P(b_{ij}) - P(a_{ij}) P(b_i) - P(a_{ij}) P(b_j)$$
$$+ P(a_{ij}) P(b_{ij}) = P(a_ib_i) + P(a_ib_j) + P(a_jb_i) + P(a_jb_j)$$
$$- P(a_ib_{ij}) - P(a_jb_{ij}) - P(a_{ij}b_i) - P(a_{ij}b_j) + P(a_{ij}b_{ij}).$$

The direct correspondence of the terms on the left and right sides of equation (3.5a) can be seen immediately. Thus, if the following conditions are true, equation (3.5) must be true.

Condition 1:

$$P(a_i) P(b_i) = P(a_ib_i)$$
$$P(a_i) P(b_j) = P(a_ib_j)$$
$$P(a_j) P(b_i) = P(a_jb_i)$$
$$P(a_j) P(b_j) = P(a_jb_j)$$

Condition 2:

$$P(a_i) P(b_{ij}) = P(a_ib_{ij})$$
$$P(a_j) P(b_{ij}) = P(a_jb_{ij})$$
$$P(a_{ij}) P(b_i) = P(a_{ij}b_i)$$
$$P(a_{ij}) P(b_j) = P(a_{ij}b_j)$$
$$P(a_{ij}) P(b_{ij}) = P(a_{ij}b_{ij}).$$

Stating $P(ab)$ in terms of its component parts makes it obvious that the left side of equation (3.5) can equal the right side of (3.5) even if some of the parts of conditions 1 and 2 are not fulfilled. That is, if positive deviations for some terms are offset by negative deviations for other terms, $P(ab)$ may equal $P(a) P(b)$. Thus, the necessary and sufficient condition is

Condition 3:

$$[P(a_i) + P(a_j) - P(a_{ij})] [P(b_i) + P(b_j) - P(b_{ij})] = P(a_ib_i)$$
$$+ P(a_ib_j) + P(a_jb_i) + P(a_jb_j) - P(a_ib_{ij}) - P(a_jb_{ij}) - P(a_{ij}b_i)$$
$$- P(a_{ij}b_j) + P(a_{ij}b_{ij}).$$

The entire discussion can easily be extended to n holdings and m motives if more general notation is used. For example, let

H_k = holdings $(k = 1, 2, 3, \ldots, n)$,

M_j = motives $(j = 1, 2, 3, \ldots, m)$, and

$2_j, 3_j \ldots, m_j$ = any combination of 2, 3, \ldots, or m motives.

Then, the proportion owning any holding (H_k) is

$$(1) \qquad P(H_k) = \Sigma P(H_k)_j - \Sigma P(H_k)_{2j} + - \ldots \pm P(H_k)_{mj}.$$

Since the general statement of independence of n items is

(2) $$P(H_k, H_{k+1}, \ldots, H_n) = P(H_k)\, P(H_{k+1}) \ldots P(H_n),$$

the proportion owning any combination of n holdings for m motives is[82]

(3) $$P(H_{kj}H_{k+1}, \ldots, H_n) = \left[\Sigma P(H_k)_j - \Sigma P(H_k)_{2j} + - \ldots \pm P(H_k)_{mj}\right]$$
$$\left[\Sigma P(H_{k+1})_j - \Sigma P(H_{k+1})_{2j} + - \ldots\right.$$
$$\left.\pm P(H_{k+1})_{mj}\right] \ldots \left[\Sigma P(H_n)_j - \Sigma P(H_n)_{2j}\right.$$
$$\left.+ - \ldots \pm P(H_n)_{mj}\right].$$

Conditions 1 through 3 can now be written as follows.

Conditions 1 and 2:
$$P(H_k, H_{k+1}, \ldots, H_n)_j = P(H_k)_j\, P(H_{k+1})_j \ldots P(H_n)_j$$
$$\ldots$$
$$P(H_k, H_{k+1}, \ldots, H_n)_{mj} = P(H_k)_{mj}\, P(H_{k+1})_{mj} \ldots P(H_n)_{mj}.$$

Condition 3:
$$P(H_k, H_{k+1}, \ldots, H_n) = \left[\Sigma P(H_k)_j - \Sigma P(H_k)_{2j} + - \ldots \pm P(H_k)_{mj}\right]$$
$$\left[\Sigma P(H_{k+1})_j - \Sigma P(H_{k+1})_{2j} + - \ldots\right.$$
$$\left.\pm P(H_{k+1})_{mj}\right] \ldots \left[\Sigma P(H_n)_j - \Sigma P(H_n)_{2j}\right.$$
$$\left.+ - \ldots \pm P(H_n)_{mj}\right].$$

---

[82] There is no simple statement for the left side of equation (3) similar to equation (1).

305337137W